Authors
Robert Pavlik
Richard G. Ramsey

Great Source Education Group
a Houghton Mifflin Company

Authors

Richard G. Ramsey is currently a national educational consultant for many schools throughout the country and serves as President of Ramsey's Communications. For more than twenty-three years he has served as a teacher and a principal for grades 1–12. Dr. Ramsey has also served on the Curriculum Frameworks Committee for the State of Florida. A lifelong teacher and educator and former principal, he is now a nationally known speaker on improving student achievement and motivating students.

Robert Pavlik taught high school English and reading for seven years. His university assignments in Colorado and Wisconsin have included teaching secondary/content area reading, chairing a Reading/Language Arts Department, and directing a Reading/Learning Center. He is an author of several books and articles and serves as the Director of the School Design and Development Center at Marquette University.

Printed in the United States of America.

International Standard Book Number: 0-47632-3

1 2 3 4 5 6 7 8 9 10 — BA — 07 06 05 04 03 02 01 00

Table of Contents

READING
AND
WRITING
Sourcebook
LEATHER · SUEDE · TAILORING

Responding to Literature

How can you be sure of understanding what you read? One way is to read actively, with a pen in hand, and mark up the text. Highlight parts that you like or ones you'd like to reread. Take notes. Write your questions down. And, make a special point to think about how what you are reading connects to <u>your</u> life.

Read this brief poem. Notice how one reader has marked it up.

RESPONSE NOTES

"I'm Nobody" by Emily Dickinson

Is she serious?

I'm nobody! Who are you?
Are you nobody too?
Then there's a pair of us—don't tell!
They'd banish us, you know.

= send us away

How dreary to be somebody!
How public, like a frog
To tell your name the livelong day
To an admiring bog.

kind of funny, but serious

VOCABULARY

banish—force someone to leave the country; force to go away.
livelong—whole length of; entire.
bog—area of soft, wet, spongy ground; marsh.

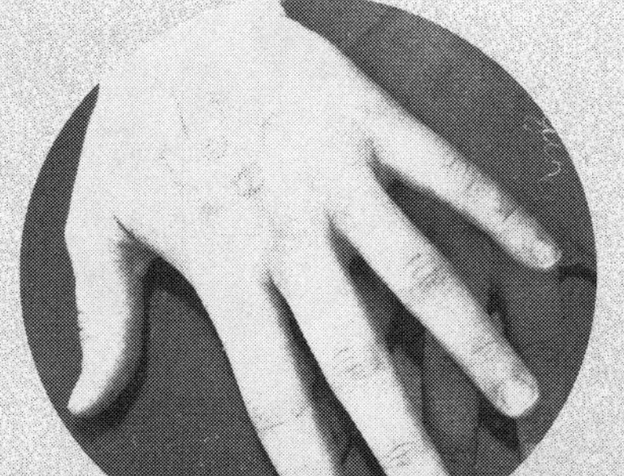

Response Strategies

Active readers mark up texts in many different ways. Each reader marks up a text a little differently, depending on what is best for him or her. How do you respond to literature? Think of it as talking with a text or author. Try to respond in any of the 6 general ways.

1. Mark or Highlight
With a pen or highlighter, underline or circle words that are important or seem confusing. By marking up a text, you set off important parts and make these parts easier to find when you come back to reread or review.

2. Question
Ask yourself questions as you read, such as, "Do I believe this?" and "Is this true?" This is a way of talking with the author. It triggers thoughts in your mind and makes your reading more meaningful.

3. Clarify
"What is the author trying to say? What does he or she mean?" You probably ask questions like this as you read. As readers, we are always trying to make clear to ourselves what we have read. Sometimes we might number or label parts of a text to keep track of points or of events or to make connections from one page to another.

4. Visualize
What do you see as you read? What images come to mind? To help you remember these mental pictures, draw what you see. You may want to draw a picture or sketch or simply make a chart. Almost any way of visualizing is useful.

5. Predict
Another way of responding to literature is to guess what will happen next. "How will this story come out in the end?" Readers naturally make predictions as they read. Guessing what will come next helps you follow the story or article more closely and get more from what you are reading.

6. React and Connect
Readers often express their opinions or jot notes and comments in the margins of books. This is another way of getting more from your reading. It helps you state your own views by recording them as you read.

Use the response strategies in the Response Notes space beside each selection in this *Sourcebook*. Look back at these examples whenever you need to.

Now practice using some of the strategies yourself. Use the poem below to try reading actively. Read the poem 2 or 3 times. Use a different response strategy each time you reread the poem.

"My Hard Repair Job" by James Berry

In the awful quarrel
we had, my temper burnt
our friendship to cinders.
How can I make it whole again?

This way, that way,
that time, this time,
I pick up the burnt bits,
trying to change them back.

VOCABULARY
cinders—burned pieces of wood or coal.

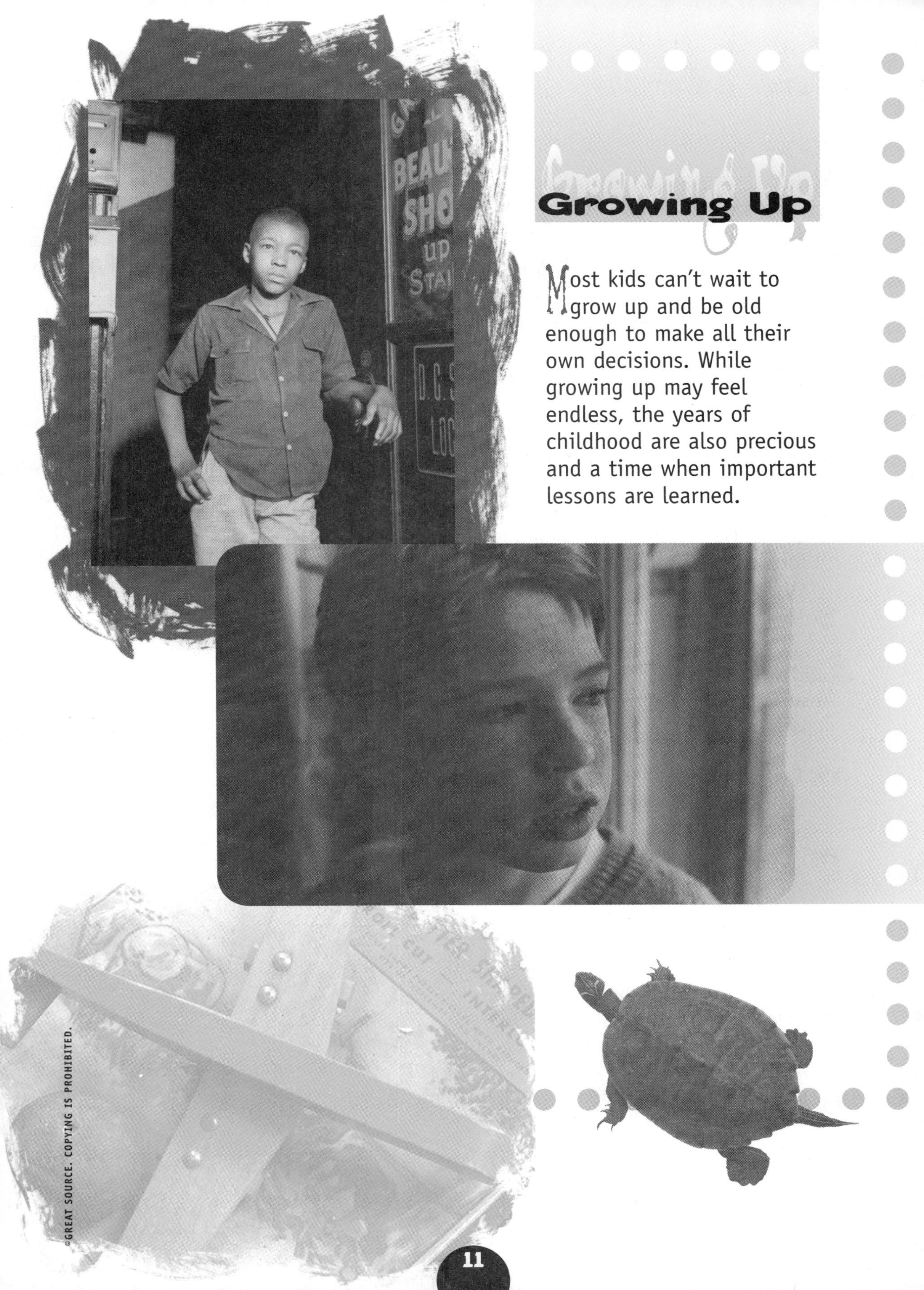

Growing Up

Most kids can't wait to grow up and be old enough to make all their own decisions. While growing up may feel endless, the years of childhood are also precious and a time when important lessons are learned.

1: The Turtle

Would you be surprised to learn that good readers are also good writers? This is because writing and reading go together, like two halves of a whole. While your eyes are reading, your hand can be circling, underlining, and making notes. While you are writing, your eyes are searching, scanning, and skimming for information.

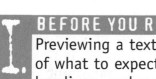

I. BEFORE YOU READ

Previewing a text before you begin gives you an idea of what to expect. In a preview, you look at the art, headings, and words that stand out.

1. Thumb quickly through "The Turtle."
2. Look closely at the art, headings, and vocabulary footnotes. Also read the questions that interrupt the story.
3. Then make some notes on this Preview Card.

Preview Card

Answer these questions as best you can. If you don't know an answer, make a guess.

WHO IS THE STORY ABOUT?

WHAT DO YOU KNOW ABOUT THE MAIN CHARACTERS?

WHERE DOES THE STORY TAKE PLACE?

WHEN DOES IT TAKE PLACE?

WHAT DO YOU PREDICT WILL BE THE PROBLEM IN THE STORY?

II. READ

Now read Jim Bishop's story. Read with a pencil and highlighter in hand.

1. **Highlight** or **mark** phrases and sentences that might be important.
2. Note comments in the Response Notes.

"The Turtle" by Jim Bishop

There had been toys around the house before. Many of them. But little Dennis loved the twenty-five-cent turtle more than the Erector sets, the book of games, the orange scooter, or the baseball mitt. The turtle was about as big as a coin. On his brown shell was his name: Oscar.

Dennis loved him and Dennis was eight years old. He saved for a ninety-eight-cent goldfish bowl and he packed small brightly colored stones in it, so that when water was added, Oscar had his own private beach. Then he placed Oscar and the bowl on a window ledge in his room so that the afternoon sun warmed the cold wrinkles in the turtle's legs and moved him, now and then, to slip and slide down the stones into the cool clear water.

When Dennis came in from school, he hurried to his room to see what Oscar was doing. Oscar was the first live thing that Dennis had ever owned.

One afternoon, Dennis hurried up the stairs and found Oscar on his back floating. As

Response Notes

EXAMPLE:
Strange that the author keeps saying how much Dennis loved the turtle.

VOCABULARY

scooter—vehicle with a long footboard between two small end wheels and a steering handle.
wrinkles—creases; lines.

young as he was, Dennis understood the finality of death. His shoulders shook and his breath caught and a wail came from his lips.

His mother hurried upstairs. She saw her little boy standing, arms hanging straight down, chin on chest, and she heard the sobs. She knew the genuine sound and she stood in front of him and held him to her breast. It took her a moment to find out what the trouble was.

He was promised a new turtle if he would stop crying. It didn't help. The crying continued and no promise on her part could slow the sobs.

stop + think

Why is Dennis crying?

She phoned her husband at his office. He was irritable. He had a business to conduct. He got into his car and came home. He hurried straight up to Dennis's room and put his arm around his boy.

"You can cry as long as you like," he said softly, "but it will not bring Oscar back. When God calls us it means that He loves us so much that He cannot bear to be apart from us any

VOCABULARY

finality—conclusiveness; completeness.
wail—cry.
irritable—easily annoyed.
conduct—do.

"The Turtle" continued

Response Notes

longer. God must have loved Oscar a great deal."

The sobbing continued. The father kept talking quietly, insistently and inexorably. "Coming home, I kept saying to myself, 'Well, now that Oscar is dead we should be asking ourselves what we can do to show him how much we love him.' Crying isn't the answer. It won't bring him back, son. What I think we ought to do is to have a funeral service for Oscar."

stop + think

Is Dennis's father a caring or uncaring person? Explain your opinion.

The sobbing began to slow. The boy was listening. He brushed his shirt sleeve against his eyes and he tried his first few words.

"What can we do for him, Dad?"

"Personally," the father said in a tentative tone, "I think we ought to bury Oscar in the back yard. We will invite Mommy and all the children of the neighborhood and I will attend too." Dennis stopped crying. His father took a

VOCABULARY

sobbing—crying.
inexorably—persistently; repeatedly.
tentative—uncertain.

Response Notes

solid silver cigarette case from his pocket. "See this? This is Oscar's casket. He will be the only turtle in the world buried in solid silver."

The eyes of Dennis glistened. "Will we have a solemn procession?"

stop + think

Do you predict Dennis will go along with his father's plan? Why?

stop + think

"Certainly," the father said. "And I will get a big rock and chisel Oscar's name on it so that centuries from now, everybody will know that Oscar is buried there."

Dennis was smiling. He looked at the goldfish bowl in time to see Oscar flip on his stomach and swim toward shore. Dennis looked up at his father.

"Let's kill him," he said.

VOCABULARY

casket—small coffin.

solemn procession—people moving in an orderly and dignified way, as at a funeral.

chisel—carve.

stop + think

Why is the ending of "The Turtle" such a surprise?

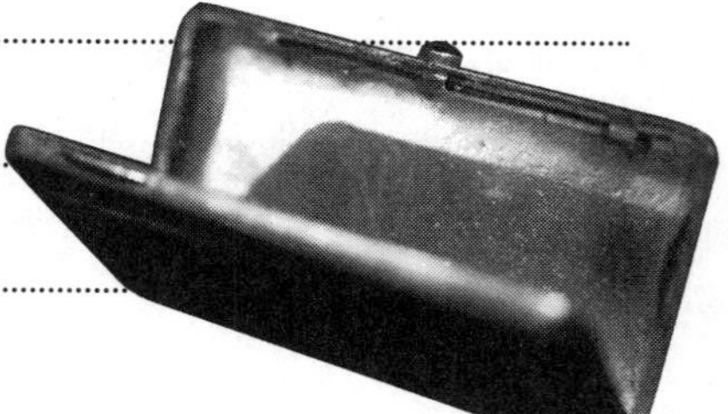

III. GATHER YOUR THOUGHTS

A. QUICKWRITE Now think of an animal you could write about. Do a 1-minute quickwrite about an animal that *is now* or *once was* important to you.

1-minute Quickwrite

B. DEVELOP YOUR IDEA Use the questions in the web diagram below to develop a paragraph about the special animal.

WHAT DOES IT LOOK LIKE?

HOW DOES IT ACT?

ANIMAL:

WHAT MAKES IT SPECIAL?

WHY DO YOU LIKE IT?

C. PLAN Study the example and then complete the graphic organizer to help you plan your paragraph.

1. Write 1 sentence that sums up why this animal is so important to you.
2. Then list 3 details that support your main idea.
3. Write a closing sentence that sums up why the animal is special to you.

Example

SUBJECT: Rover

MAIN IDEA: Rover is important to me because he keeps me company when I'm feeling alone.

DETAIL:	DETAIL:	DETAIL:
He's always there after school.	He sleeps with me during storms.	He never argues with me or makes me feel left out.

CONCLUSION: If it weren't for Rover, I'd feel pretty lonely sometimes.

SUBJECT:

MAIN IDEA:

DETAIL:	DETAIL:	DETAIL:

CONCLUSION:

IV. WRITE

Now write your **paragraph** about the animal.

1. Start with your main idea sentence.
2. Then offer 3 details that will help your readers get to know the animal. End with a closing sentence.
3. Use the Writers' Checklist to help you revise.

WRITERS' CHECKLIST

SENTENCES

- ❑ **Did all your sentences begin with capital letters?** EXAMPLE: *It was clear that Dennis loved Oscar.*
- ❑ **Did they all end with the correct punctuation?** EXAMPLE: *What are you talking about?*
- ❑ **Did every sentence express a complete thought?** EXAMPLES: *Danny and his father checking.* (incomplete) *Danny and his father checked the turtle bowl.* (complete)

V. WRAP-UP

What is the point or main idea of "The Turtle"?

READERS' CHECKLIST

UNDERSTANDING

- ❑ Did you understand the reading?
- ❑ Was the message or point clear?
- ❑ Can you restate what the reading is about?

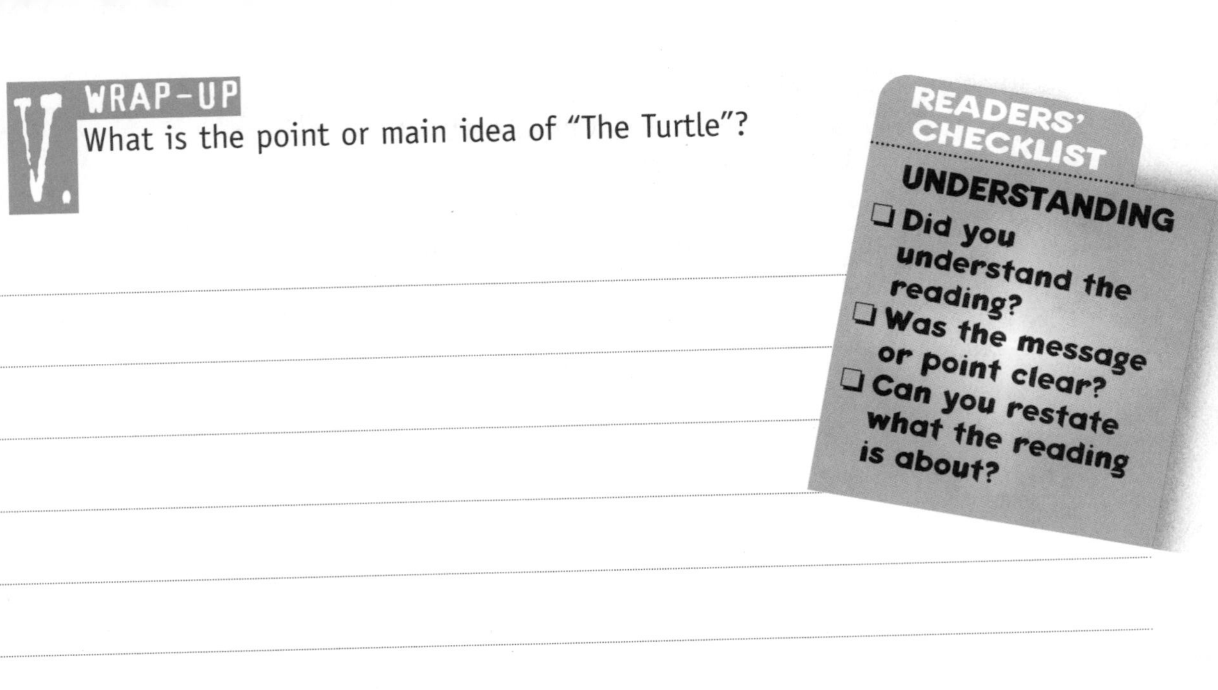

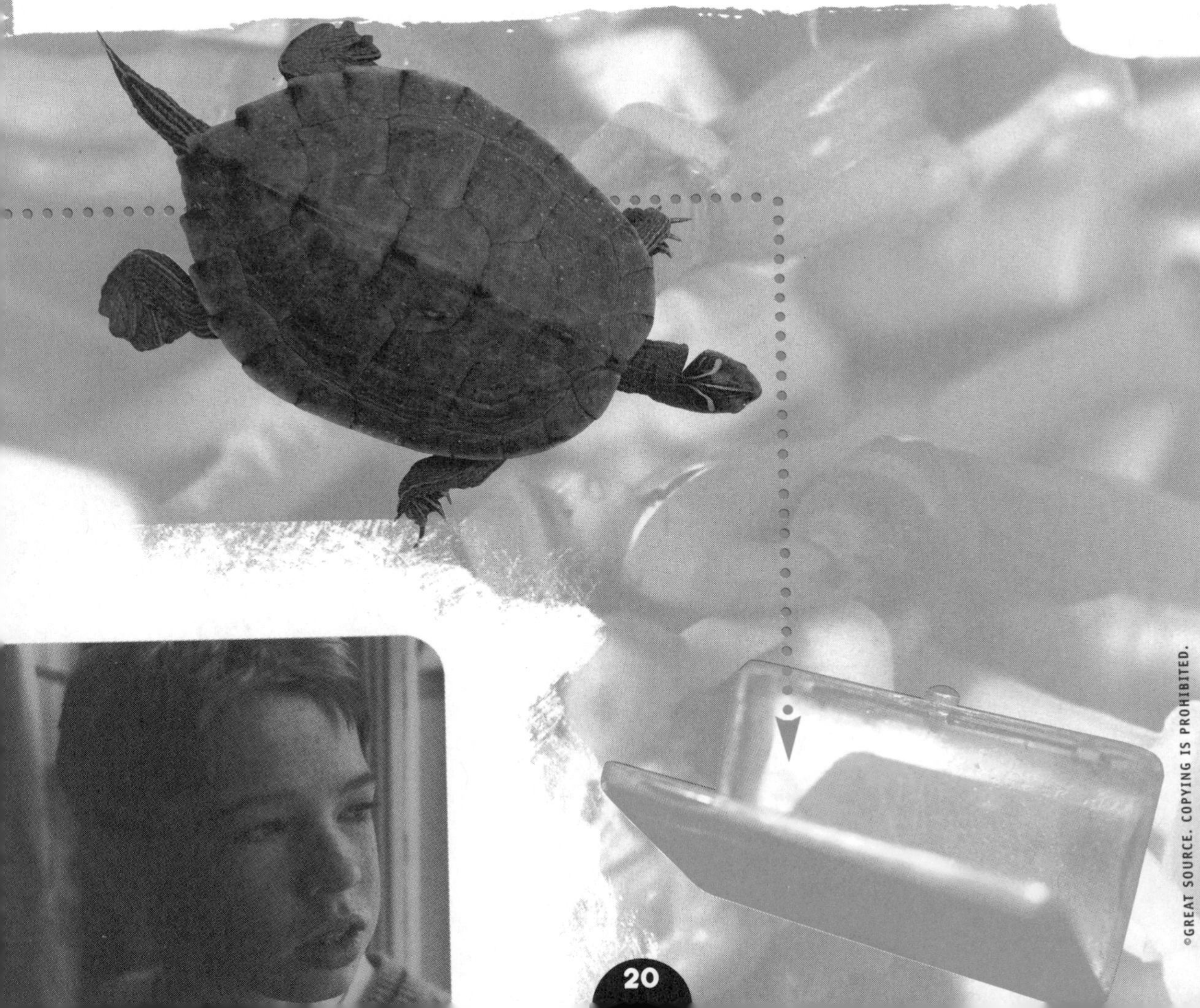

2: Thank You, Ma'am

Are you usually by yourself when you read and write? Reading and writing don't have to be done alone. Read with a friend. Write in a group. Discuss ideas. Ask each other questions. Act out scenes. Say what you think and share what you learn.

I. BEFORE YOU READ

Take turns reading each sentence below with a partner. The sentences come from the story "Thank You, Ma'am."

1. Decide which sentence comes first, which comes next, and so on. Number them.
2. Then discuss what you think the story will be about. Write your predictions below.

Think-Pair-Share

_____ "Here I am trying to get home to cook me a bite to eat, and you snatch my pocketbook!"

_____ The woman said, "You ought to be my son. I would teach you right from wrong."

_____ Then she said, "Now ain't you ashamed of yourself?"

_____ It was about eleven o'clock at night, dark, and she was walking alone, when a boy ran up behind her and tried to snatch her purse.

_____ "I want a pair of blue suede shoes," said the boy.

I predict the story will be about:

....

....

....

(circle one)

I predict the story will have a **happy / unhappy** ending.

II. READ

Now read "Thank You, Ma'am."

1. As you read, pay attention to the order of events in the story.
2. Write **predictions** about what will happen next.

Response Notes

EXAMPLE:
The woman will get very angry. . . .

"Thank You, Ma'am" by Langston Hughes

She was a large woman with a large purse that had everything in it but a hammer and nails. It had a long strap, and she carried it slung across her shoulder. It was about eleven o'clock at night, dark, and she was walking alone, when a boy ran up behind her and tried to snatch her purse. The strap broke with the sudden single tug the boy gave it from behind. But the boy's weight and the weight of the purse combined caused him to lose his balance. Instead of taking off full blast as he had hoped, the boy fell on his back on the sidewalk and his legs flew up. The large woman simply turned around and kicked him right square in his blue-jeaned sitter. Then she reached down, picked the boy up by his shirt front, and shook him until his teeth rattled.

After that, the woman said, "Pick up my pocketbook, boy, and give it here."

She still held him tightly. But she bent down enough to permit him to stoop and pick up her purse. Then she said, "Now ain't you ashamed of yourself?"

Firmly gripped by his shirt front, the boy said, "Yes'm."

VOCABULARY

permit—allow.

Response Notes

The woman said, "What did you want to do it for?"

The boy said, "I didn't aim to."

She said, "You a lie!"

By that time two or three people passed, stopped, turned to look, and some stood watching.

"If I turn you loose, will you run?" asked the woman.

"Yes'm," said the boy.

"Then I won't turn you loose," said the woman. She did not release him.

"Lady, I'm sorry," whispered the boy.

"Um-hum! Your face is dirty. I got a great mind to wash your face for you. Ain't you got nobody home to tell you to wash your face?"

"No'm," said the boy.

"Then it will get washed this evening," said the large woman, starting up the street, dragging the frightened boy behind her.

He looked as if he were fourteen or fifteen, frail and willow-wild, in tennis shoes and blue jeans.

The woman said, "You ought to be my son. I would teach you right from wrong. Least I can do right now is to wash your face. Are you hungry?"

"No'm," said the being-dragged boy. "I just want you to turn me loose."

"Was I bothering *you* when I turned that corner?" asked the woman.

VOCABULARY

frail—slender; delicate.

"No'm."

"But you put yourself in contact with *me*," said the woman. "If you think that that contact is not going to last awhile, you got another thought coming. When I get through with you, sir, you are going to remember Mrs. Luella Bates Washington Jones."

Sweat popped out on the boy's face and he began to struggle. Mrs. Jones stopped, jerked him around in front of her, put a half-nelson about his neck, and continued to drag him up the street. When she got to her door, she dragged the boy inside, down a hall, and into a large kitchenette-furnished room at the rear of the house. She switched on the light and left the door open. The boy could hear other roomers laughing and talking in the large house. Some of their doors were open, too, so he knew he and the woman were not alone. The woman still had him by the neck in the middle of her room.

Story Frame

Fill in this Story Frame about what has happened so far. What happened first? second? third?

1.

2.

3.

VOCABULARY

half-nelson—wrestling hold.
kitchenette-furnished room—room with a small kitchen.

"Thank You, Ma'am" continued

Response Notes

She said, "What is your name?"

"Roger," answered the boy.

"Then, Roger, you go to that sink and wash your face," said the woman, whereupon she turned him loose—at last. Roger looked at the door—looked at the woman—looked at the door—*and went to the sink.*

"Let the water run until it gets warm," she said. "Here's a clean towel."

"You gonna take me to jail?" asked the boy, bending over the sink.

"Not with that face, I would not take you nowhere," said the woman. "Here I am trying to get home to cook me a bite to eat, and you snatch my pocketbook! Maybe you ain't been to your supper either, late as it be. Have you?"

"There's nobody home at my house," said the boy.

"Then we'll eat," said the woman. "I believe you're hungry—or been hungry—to try to snatch my pocketbook!"

"I want a pair of blue suede shoes," said the boy.

"Well, you didn't have to snatch *my* pocketbook to get some suede shoes," said Mrs. Luella Bates Washington Jones. "You could of asked me."

"Ma'am?"

The water dripping from his face, the boy looked at her. There was a long pause. A very long pause. After he had dried his face and not

VOCABULARY

snatch—grab.
suede—soft leather.

knowing what else to do, dried it again, the boy turned around, wondering what next. The door was open. He could make a dash for it down the hill. He could run, run, run, *run!*

The woman was sitting on the day bed. After a while she said, "I were young once and I wanted things I could not get."

There was another long pause. The boy's mouth opened. Then he frowned, not knowing he frowned.

The woman said, "Um-hum! You thought I was going to say *but*, didn't you? You thought I was going to say, *but I didn't snatch people's pocketbooks*. Well, I wasn't going to say that." Pause. Silence. "I have done things, too, which I would not tell you, son—neither tell God, if He didn't already know. Everybody's got something in common. So you set down while I fix us something to eat. You might run that comb through your hair so you will look presentable."

Story Frame

Continue the Story Frame you started on page 24. List the next 3 things that happened in the story.

4.

5.

6.

VOCABULARY

frowned—looked unhappy.
presentable—nice enough to be seen by others; proper.

Response Notes

In another corner of the room behind a screen was a gas plate and an icebox. Mrs. Jones got up and went behind the screen. The woman did not watch the boy to see if he was going to run now, nor did she watch her purse, which she left behind her on the day bed. But the boy took care to sit on the far side of the room, away from the purse, where he thought she could easily see him out of the corner of her eye if she wanted to. He did not trust the woman *not* to trust him. And he did not want to be mistrusted now.

"Do you need somebody to go to the store," asked the boy, "maybe to get some milk or something?"

"Don't believe I do," said the woman, "unless you just want sweet milk yourself. I was going to make cocoa out of this canned milk I got here."

"That will be fine," said the boy.

She heated some lima beans and ham she had in the icebox, made the cocoa, and set the table. The woman did not ask the boy anything about where he lived, or his folks, or anything else that would embarrass him. Instead, as they ate, she told him about her job in a hotel beauty shop that stayed open late, what the work was like, and how all kinds of women

VOCABULARY

cocoa—chocolate drink.
lima beans—large light green beans.
embarrass—discomfort.

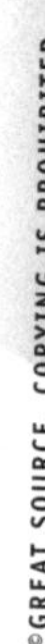

came in and out, blondes, redheads, and Spanish. Then she cut him a half of her ten-cent cake.

"Eat some more, son," she said.

When they were finished eating, she got up and said, "Now here, take this ten dollars and buy yourself sonic blue suede shoes. And next time, do not make the mistake of latching onto my pocketbook nor nobody else's—because shoes got by devilish ways will burn your feet. I got to get my rest now. But from here on in, son, I hope you will behave yourself."

She led him down the hall to the front door and opened it. "Good night! Behave yourself, boy!" she said, looking out into the street as he went down the steps.

The boy wanted to say something other than, "Thank you, ma'am," to Mrs. Luella Bates Washington Jones, but although his lips moved, he couldn't even say that as he turned at the foot of the barren stoop and looked up at the large woman in the door. Then she shut the door.

VOCABULARY

sonic blue suede shoes—particular kind of popular, fancy shoes.
Behave—act properly.
barren stoop—plain front porch.

Story Frame

Complete this Story Frame for "Thank You, Ma'am." Share and discuss what you wrote with a partner.

THE STORY TAKES PLACE IN

________________ IS A CHARACTER IN THE STORY WHO

________________ IS ANOTHER CHARACTER WHO

A PROBLEM OCCURS WHEN

AFTER THAT

THE PROBLEM IS SOLVED WHEN

THE STORY ENDS WITH

III. GATHER YOUR THOUGHTS

A. RECALL PLOT Think about the plot of "Thank You, Ma'am." Then list, in order, the 4 most important things that happen in the story.

1. ______

2. ______

3. ______

4. ______

B. PLAN Now think of a time when someone taught you right from wrong. Complete the sentences below to help you plan a paragraph about the experience.

When I was ______ years old, I ______.

When my ______ found out, he/she ______

______ and ______.

Later, he/she ______.

I felt ______.

The whole thing was resolved when I ______

______.

Afterwards, I decided ______

______.

IV. WRITE

Now write a **narrative paragraph** about the time someone taught you right from wrong.

1. Write in the first-person (*I said, we thought*).
2. Use your notes from the previous page to keep your narrative brief and to the point.
3. Use the Writers' Checklist to help you revise.

WRITERS' CHECKLIST

SENTENCE FRAGMENTS

❏ **Did you use only complete sentences in your writing? A complete sentence contains a subject and a verb and expresses a complete thought. A sentence fragment, on the other hand, may look and sound like a sentence, but it is somehow incomplete. You can fix a sentence fragment by adding a subject or a verb, taking out words, or combining the fragment with another sentence.**

EXAMPLES: *Standing on the corner. (fragment)*
The boy was standing on the corner. (complete sentence)
Because Mrs. Jones was kind. (fragment)
Because Mrs. Jones was kind, she helped the boy. (complete sentence)

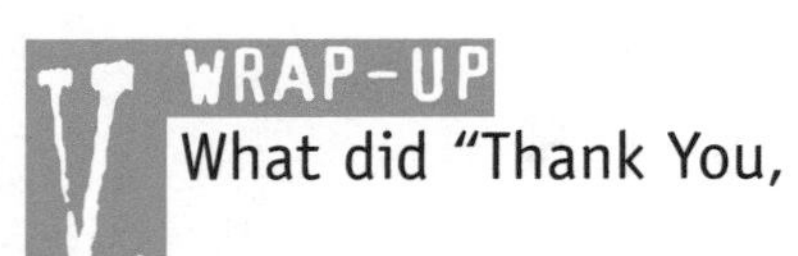

V. WRAP-UP

What did "Thank You, Ma'am" mean to you?

READERS' CHECKLIST

MEANING

- ❑ Did you learn something from the reading?
- ❑ Did it affect you or make an impression?

Abraham Lincoln

John Wilkes Booth

A Civil War hospital

The Civil War (1861–1865) was one of the bloodiest wars in American history. It bitterly divided the country, pitting brother against brother and North against South. The Northern states fought to end slavery, while the Southern states battled to preserve slavery. Although the North triumphed in the end, victory came at a high price.

3: Caring for the Wounded

Sometimes you don't need to read every word of a book or article. Glance through it quickly. Skimming can help you quickly find the information you need.

I. BEFORE YOU READ

Read the questions below.

1. Then skim "Caring for the Wounded." Don't read every word. Instead, look only for words and phrases that can help you answer the questions.
2. Write your answers below.

SKIMMING

Who was Clara Barton?

When did she live?

What did she do?

Why was her work so important?

II. READ

Now read Barton's memoir.

1. As you read, **visualize** (make a mental picture of) the people and places she describes.
2. Draw a sketch in the Response Notes each time you get a clear picture of a person or event.

"Caring for the Wounded" by Clara Barton

RESPONSE NOTES

EXAMPLE:

About three o' clock in the morning I observed a surgeon with his little flickering candle in hand approaching me with cautious step far up in the wood. "Lady," he said as he drew near, "will you go with me? Out on the hills is a poor distressed lad, mortally wounded and dying. His piteous cries for his sister have touched all our hearts, and none of us can relieve him, but rather seem to distress him by our presence."

By this time I was following him back over the bloody track, with great beseeching eyes of anguish on every side looking up into our faces saying so plainly, "Don't step on us."

"He can't last half an hour longer," said the surgeon as we toiled on. "He is already quite cold, shot through the abdomen, a terrible wound." By this time the cries became plainly audible to me.

"Mary, Mary, sister Mary, come—oh, come, I am wounded, Mary! I am shot. I am dying—oh, come to me—I have called you so long and my

VOCABULARY

cautious—careful.
distressed—suffering.
mortally wounded—seriously hurt.
piteous—sad.
beseeching—begging.
anguish—pain.
toiled—worked.
abdomen—belly.
audible—loud enough to be heard.

RESPONSE NOTES

strength is almost gone—Don't let me die here alone. Oh, Mary, Mary, come!"

Of all the tones of entreaty to which I have listened—and certainly I have had some experience of sorrow—I think these, sounding through that dismal night, the most heart-rending.

stop and think

What has happened so far?

DRAW A PICTURE HERE OF THE SCENE BARTON DESCRIBES.

As we drew near, some 20 persons, attracted by his cries, had gathered around and stood with moistened eyes and helpless hands waiting the change which would relieve them all. And in the midst, stretched upon the ground, lay, scarcely full grown, a young man with a graceful head of hair, tangled and matted, thrown back from a forehead and a face of livid whiteness. His throat was bare. His hands,

VOCABULARY

entreaty—begging; pleading.
dismal—gloomy.
heart-rending—heart-breaking.
moistened—teary; filled with tears.
relieve—help.
livid—pale.

bloody, clasped his breast, his large, bewildered eyes turning anxiously, in every direction. And ever from between his ashen lips pealed that piteous cry of "Mary! Mary! Come."

I approached him unobserved, and, motioning the lights away, I knelt by him alone in the darkness. Shall I confess that I intended if possible to cheat him out of his terrible death agony? But my lips were truer than my heart, and would not speak the word "Brother" I had willed them to do. So I placed my hands upon his neck, kissed his cold forehead, and laid my cheek against his.

The illusion was complete; the act had done the falsehood my lips refused to speak. I can never forget that cry of joy. "Oh, Mary! Mary! You have come? I knew you would come if I called you and I have called you so long. I could not die without you, Mary. Don't cry, darling, I am not afraid to die now that you have come to me. Oh, bless you. Bless you, Mary." And he ran his cold, blood-wet hands about my neck, passed them over my face, and twined them in my hair, which by this time had freed itself from fastenings and was hanging damp and heavy upon my shoulders.

He gathered the loose locks in his stiffened fingers and holding them to his lips continued to whisper through them, "Bless you, bless you, Mary!" And I felt the hot tears of joy trickling from the eyes I had thought stony in death. This

RESPONSE NOTES

VOCABULARY

bewildered—puzzled.
ashen—very pale.
pealed—sounded loudly.
illusion—false impression.
locks—strands of hair.

RESPONSE NOTES

encouraged me, and, wrapping his feet closely in blankets and giving him such stimulants as he could take, I seated myself on the ground and lifted him on my lap, and drawing the shawl on my own shoulders also about his I bade him rest.

stop AND retell

What does Barton do to calm the wounded soldier?

I listened till his blessings grew fainter, and in 10 minutes with them on his lips he fell asleep. So the gray morning found us; my precious charge had grown warm, and was comfortable.

Of course the morning light would reveal his mistake. But he had grown calm and was refreshed and able to endure it, and when finally he woke, he seemed puzzled for a moment, but then he smiled and said: "I knew before I opened my eyes that this couldn't be Mary. I know now that she couldn't get here, but it is almost as good. You've made me so happy. Who is it?"

I said it was simply a lady who, hearing that he was wounded, had come to care for him. He

VOCABULARY

stimulants—enlivening things, such as food or drink.
bade—wished.
fainter—weaker.
charge—person cared for by another.

"Caring for the Wounded" CONTINUED

RESPONSE NOTES

wanted the name, and with childlike simplicity he spelled it letter by letter to know if he were right. "In my pocket," he said, "you will find mother's last letter; please get it and write your name upon it, for I want both names by me when I die."

VOCABULARY
simplicity—innocence.

stop AND retell

What have you learned about Clara Barton? Explain.

What have you learned about medical treatment during the Civil War?

Clara Barton

III. GATHER YOUR THOUGHTS

A. NARROW YOUR FOCUS When you retell an event, you don't tell everything. You zoom in on the most important parts and keep your focus there. Practice narrowing your focus.

1. In the center circle below, write a few sentences describing what your day was like yesterday.
2. Then, in each of the surrounding circles write a specific event that happened yesterday.

I took a 2-hour placement test for high school.

BROAD STATEMENT ABOUT YOUR DAY

Yesterday was long and busy. I got up at 6 and kept going and going until 11 pm!

I met Raf and Andre at the mall after school.

I helped Mom change her tire in the pitch dark.

B. DEVELOP THE TOPIC Now choose 1 event from the diagram above to tell about in a letter. Answer these questions about the event.

The event: ____________________

Who was involved? ____________________

What happened? ____________________

Where did it occur? ____________________

When did it happen? ____________________

Why did it happen? ____________________

IV. WRITE

Write a **letter** to a friend or relative. Retell the event you focused on in Part III.

1. Include plenty of details. Give your readers a "you are there" feeling.
2. Use the Writers' Checklist to help you revise.

(Date)

(Greeting)

Always begin with a salutation or greeting. A salutation begins with *Dear* and is followed by the name of the person receiving the letter. A comma follows the person's name.
EXAMPLE: *Dear Ruth,*

Continue your writing on the next page.

Continue your writing from the previous page.

WRITERS' CHECKLIST

LETTERS

- ❑ **Did you capitalize each word in the greeting?**
- ❑ **Did you put a comma at the end of the greeting?**
- ❑ **Did you capitalize only the first word in the closing?**
- ❑ **Did you write the date in the top right-hand corner of the letter?**

End with a closing. The closing appears two lines below the body of your letter. Only the first word is capitalized. The closing is followed by a comma.

EXAMPLES:
Sincerely yours,
With love, and
Your friend,

(Closing)

V. WRAP-UP

Did you find "Caring for the Wounded" easy or hard to read? Why?

READERS' CHECKLIST

EASE

- ❑ **Was the passage easy to read?**
- ❑ **Were you able to read it smoothly and without difficulty?**

4: The President's Been Shot

Think of all the times someone has told you to "get ready"—maybe a teacher, a coach, or a friend. Getting ready to read a story or article means thinking about what you already know about a subject and what you want to find out. A K-W-L (What I **K**now—What I **W**ant to Know—What I **L**earned) chart is an effective strategy because it helps keep information organized.

I. BEFORE YOU READ

"The President's Been Shot" is about the assassination of Abraham Lincoln. Use the K-W-L Chart to help you get ready to read the article.

1. Write what you know about Lincoln and his murder in the **K** space.
2. Write what you want to find out in the **W** space.

K-W-L CHART

K What I **K**now

W What I **W**ant to Know

L What I **L**earned

II. READ

Now read "The President's Been Shot."

1. Think about how this account of Lincoln's murder makes you feel.
2. **React** and **connect** to the article. Jot down your feelings in the Response Notes as you read.

"The President's Been Shot" by Richard Bak

RESPONSE NOTES

EXAMPLE:
Today the Secret Service would have tighter security.

It was sometime around 10:15, with the third act in progress. Booth had been in and out of the theater several times while the play was in progress, leaving to fortify himself with a stiff drink of whiskey before returning. In the alley, Edman Spangler was supposed to be holding the reins of his mare. Now, Booth's frenzied preparations earlier in the day were about to pay off. That afternoon, while the theater was empty, he had bored a finger-sized peephole in the inner door to the box. This gave him a perfect view of the back of Lincoln's rocking chair. He'd also gouged a mortise in the plaster wall opposite the door leading into the corridor. By bracing a wooden bar between the door and the wall, he was able to prevent anyone from rushing through the jammed door. From under his coat he pulled a .44-caliber derringer pistol and a nine-inch knife.

Mary Lincoln would give two different accounts of her husband's last words. At first,

VOCABULARY

fortify—strengthen.
reins of his mare—leather straps used to control a horse.
frenzied—crazed.
peephole—hole through which to look.
mortise—hole.
corridor—narrow hallway.
.44-caliber derringer pistol—gun.

"The President's Been Shot" CONTINUED

she remembered that she had been leaning close to him, her hand on his knobby knee, and said playfully, "What will Miss Harris think of my hanging on to you so?" To which Lincoln replied: "She won't think anything about it."

Her other version had the president, perhaps waking from some private daydream, improbably saying, "How I should like to visit Jerusalem sometime!"

RESPONSE NOTES

STOP AND PREDICT

What do you think Lincoln's last words were about?

In the play, comic lead Harry Hawk played Asa Trenchard, an American backwoodsman trying to pass himself off as a millionaire. Hawk was alone on the stage when he responded to the gold-digging mother who had just discovered he was as poor as a church mouse. "Don't know the manners of good society, eh?" he said. "Well, I guess I know enough to turn you inside out, old gal—you sockdologizing old mantrap!"

Hawk was looking in Mrs. Lincoln's direction as he delivered the lines. He would always remember that she was smiling at the very moment a shot rang out in the president's box.

VOCABULARY

knobby—round and bony.
backwoodsman—person from a remote area.
gold-digging—wanting to marry for money.
sockdologizing old mantrap—loud-mouthed woman who wants to catch a husband.

stop and clarify

Who was Mr. Hawk, and what was he doing at the time Lincoln was shot?

RESPONSE NOTES

"The President's Been Shot" CONTINUED

Long seconds of quiet bewilderment were followed by outright pandemonium. Edwin Emerson was standing in the wings, waiting for his cue to go on, when he heard the *cra-a-ck!* of a pistol. He described the delayed reaction and ensuing chaos:

I was not surprised, nor was anyone else behind the scenes. Such sounds are too common during the shifting of the various sets to surprise an actor. For a good many seconds after that sound nothing happened behind the footlights. Then, as I stood there in the dimness, a man rushed by me, making for the stage door. I did not recognize Booth at the time, nor did anyone else, I think, unless perhaps someone out on the stage, when he stood a moment and shouted with theatrical gesture, "Sic Semper Tyrannis! *(So perish all tyrants!)*"

VOCABULARY

bewilderment—confusion.
pandemonium—uproar; confusion.
footlights—lights placed in a row along the front of the stage.

stop and summarize

What happened immediately after Lincoln was shot?

"The President's Been Shot" CONTINUED

Even after he flashed by, there was quiet for a few moments among the actors and the stage hands. No one knew what had happened.

Then the fearful cry, springing from nowhere it seemed, ran like wildfire behind the scenes:

"The President's shot!"

RESPONSE NOTES

?? STOP AND QUESTION ??

Write 3 questions you would like to ask the author about how and when President Lincoln was shot.

1.

2.

3.

Next return to your K-W-L Chart on page 43. Write what you learned in the **L** space.

III. GATHER YOUR THOUGHTS

A. WRITE A TOPIC SENTENCE The topic of an article is what the article's all about. Write a sentence that tells the topic of "The President's Been Shot."

TOPIC SENTENCE

"The President's Been Shot" is about

B. SUMMARIZE DETAILS The details in an article help you understand the *who, what, where, when,* and *why* of the topic. List 5 details from the article that you can include in a summary you will write.

DETAILS

1.

2.

3.

4.

5.

C. WRITE A CLOSING SENTENCE Finish off your summary paragraph with a sentence that restates the main point.

CLOSING SENTENCE

IV. WRITE

Use your notes on the previous page to write a brief **summary** of "The President's Been Shot."

1. Begin with a topic sentence.
2. Then give the most important details—names, times, places, and events from the selection.
3. Finish with a closing sentence that ties all your points together.
4. Use the Writers' Checklist to help you revise.

WRITERS' CHECKLIST

RUN-ON SENTENCES

❑ **Did you avoid run-on sentences? The two parts of a compound sentence must be joined by a comma and a conjunction, such as *and*, *but*, or *so*. A compound sentence that is missing the conjunction and the comma is called a run-on sentence.** EXAMPLE: ***I heard about Lincoln he was shot.*** **You can fix a run-on sentence by breaking it apart into two sentences (*I heard about Lincoln. He was shot.*) or by inserting a comma and a conjunction in the correct spot. (*I learned about Lincoln, and he was shot.*)**

V. WRAP-UP

What did you like best about "The President's Been Shot"?

READERS' CHECKLIST

ENJOYMENT

- ❑ **Did you like the reading?**
- ❑ **Was the reading experience pleasurable?**
- ❑ **Would you want to reread the piece or recommend it to someone?**

Paul Fleischman

Paul Fleischman was born in Monterey, California. He has written numerous books for young readers. In 1989, he won the Newbery Medal for his book of poems, *Joyful Noise*. Much of Fleischman's work reflects his keen interest in nature and American history.

5: Toby Boyce and Gideon Adams

How is going shopping like reading? Let's say you want to buy a new sweater. Do you go right to the first rack, grab a sweater, and take it to the cashier? No, you walk through the store and see what's there. When you read, walk through the selection first, so you know what to expect.

I. BEFORE YOU READ

Thumb through "Toby Boyce" and "Gideon Adams."

1. Look for names of people and places and at the pictures.
2. Then answer the questions below.

WALK-THROUGH

Who is the author?

What character names did you notice?

What place names did you notice?

What pictures did you find interesting or unusual?

What do you think these selections will be about?

READ

Now read "Toby Boyce" and "Gideon Adams."

1. As you read, think of **questions** about the characters that you would like to ask the author.
2. Write your questions in the Response Notes.

"Toby Boyce" from *Bull Run*
by Paul Fleischman

I was eleven years old and desperate to kill a Yankee before the supply ran out. It seemed that all Georgia had joined except me. I knew I'd never pass for eighteen. You can't very well lie about your height. Then I heard that musicians were needed to play for the soldiers, any age at all. I hotfooted it fifteen miles to the courthouse and took my place in line. The recruiter scowled when I reached the front. "You're a knee baby yet," he said. "Go on home." I told him I meant to join the band. "And what would your instrument be?" he asked. My thinking hadn't traveled that far. "The fife," I spoke out. Which was a monstrous lie. He smiled at me and I felt limp with relief. Then he stood up and ambled out the door. Across from the courthouse a band had begun playing. We all heard the music stop of a sudden. A few minutes later the recruiter returned. He held out a fife. "Give us 'Dixie,'" he said. I felt hot all over. Everyone

RESPONSE NOTES

EXAMPLE:
Did his parents know what he was doing?

VOCABULARY

desperate—ready to run any risk.
Yankee—soldier fighting for the North.
hotfooted—hurried.
recruiter—person in charge of getting people to join the army.
scowled—frowned.
fife—small, high-pitched musical instrument similar to the flute.
limp—weak.
ambled—walked slowly.

RESPONSE NOTES

waited. The fife seemed to burn and writhe in my hand like the Devil's own tail. I heard Grandpap saying, as he had heaps of times, "A lie is a weed in the Lord's flower garden."

DOUBLE-ENTRY JOURNAL

In the right-hand column, write down your reactions to and ideas about the quote in the left-hand column.

QUOTE	MY RESPONSE (MY THOUGHTS AND FEELINGS)
"I heard Grandpap saying, as he had heaps of times, 'A lie is a weed in the Lord's flower garden.'"	

Then that left my mind and I recollected him saying "Faith sows miracles." I found what seemed to be the mouth hole. "'Dixie,'" I announced. I closed my eyes. Then I commenced to blow and wag my fingers, singing out the song strong in my head. I believed it was coming from the fife as well, until I saw the faces around me. One man had his jacket over his head. The room echoed a considerable time after I'd finished playing. The recruiter's eyes opened slow as a frog's. I was surprised at his expression. "You've got spirit," he said at last. "And boldness. And pluck enough, I judge, to practice almighty

VOCABULARY

writhe—twist.
commenced—began.
expression—look on his face.
pluck—courage.
almighty—powerfully.

hard, *starting today.*" It was the first miracle I'd ever seen.

DOUBLE-ENTRY JOURNAL

In the right-hand column, record your ideas about the quotation.

QUOTE	MY RESPONSE (MY THOUGHTS AND FEELINGS)
"It was the first miracle I'd ever seen."	

RESPONSE NOTES

"Gideon Adams" from *Bull Run*

by Paul Fleischman

The next day four of us marched to a recruiting tent to join the infantry. I happened to be the first in line. The enlisting officer had just asked me to sign when he noticed the hair curling out from my cap, saw for the first time that I was a Negro, and informed me in the most impolite terms that I could not be admitted as a soldier.

We left, despairing of ever fighting the South. Some of the men I knew put their pride in their pockets and joined as ditchdiggers. Some signed on as cooks or teamsters. Some

VOCABULARY

miracle—amazing and marvelous thing.
infantry—army.
impolite—rude.
despairing—losing all hope.
ditchdiggers—people who dug ditches in the ground, creating a defensive fort for the fighting soldiers.
teamsters—people who carried supplies.

RESPONSE NOTES

stayed home, to hear once more that Negroes were cowardly, lazy, disloyal. I, however, refused to resign myself to serving with shovel or spoon. I would stand at the front of the fray, not the rear, and would hold a rifle in my hand. That recruiter had shown me the way.

DOUBLE-ENTRY JOURNAL

Write your questions and ideas about the quote.

QUOTE	MY RESPONSE (MY THOUGHTS AND FEELINGS)
"I, however, refused to resign myself to serving with shovel or spoon. I would stand at the front of the fray. . . ."	

I clipped my hair short that very night. The next day, I bought a bigger cap, one with a chin strap to hold it in place. Then I walked to a different recruiting station. The enlisting officer asked me my name. I foolishly feared he might recognize it. I looked up at a banner that read "One Thousand Able-Bodied Patriots Wanted," and gave him "Able" in place of "Adams." His brows furrowed at my fumbling reply. He asked me my age, then whether I'd any physical infirmities. He then asked what

VOCABULARY

fray—fighting.
furrowed—wrinkled.
physical infirmities—health problems.

manner of service I intended. "Infantry soldier," I firmly replied. Perhaps I'd spoken too firmly. He studied me. I wondered if my cap had slipped. He said I'd be paid thirteen dollars a month and that the regiment would serve ninety days, time enough to whip the Rebels three times over, he assured me. He put his finger on a line in his roll book. I nearly signed my real name, and clumsily corrected myself. I stared at the letters. I was no longer who I was. The recruiter told me to return the next morning. I left in a daze, glancing at the white men around me, who thought me one of them. The dread of discovery streaked through my veins. I gave my chin strap a tightening tug.

RESPONSE NOTES

VOCABULARY

regiment—military unit of troops.
daze—state of confusion.

DOUBLE-ENTRY JOURNAL

After carefully thinking about the 2 quotes below, write down your response to each.

QUOTES	MY RESPONSE (MY THOUGHTS AND FEELINGS)
1. "I was no longer who I was."	
2. "The dread of discovery streaked through my veins."	

III. GATHER YOUR THOUGHTS

A. UNDERSTAND A CHARACTER Write the name of either Toby Boyce or Gideon Adams in the center of the cluster. In the surrounding circles, write an adjective (a descriptive word) that describes the character.

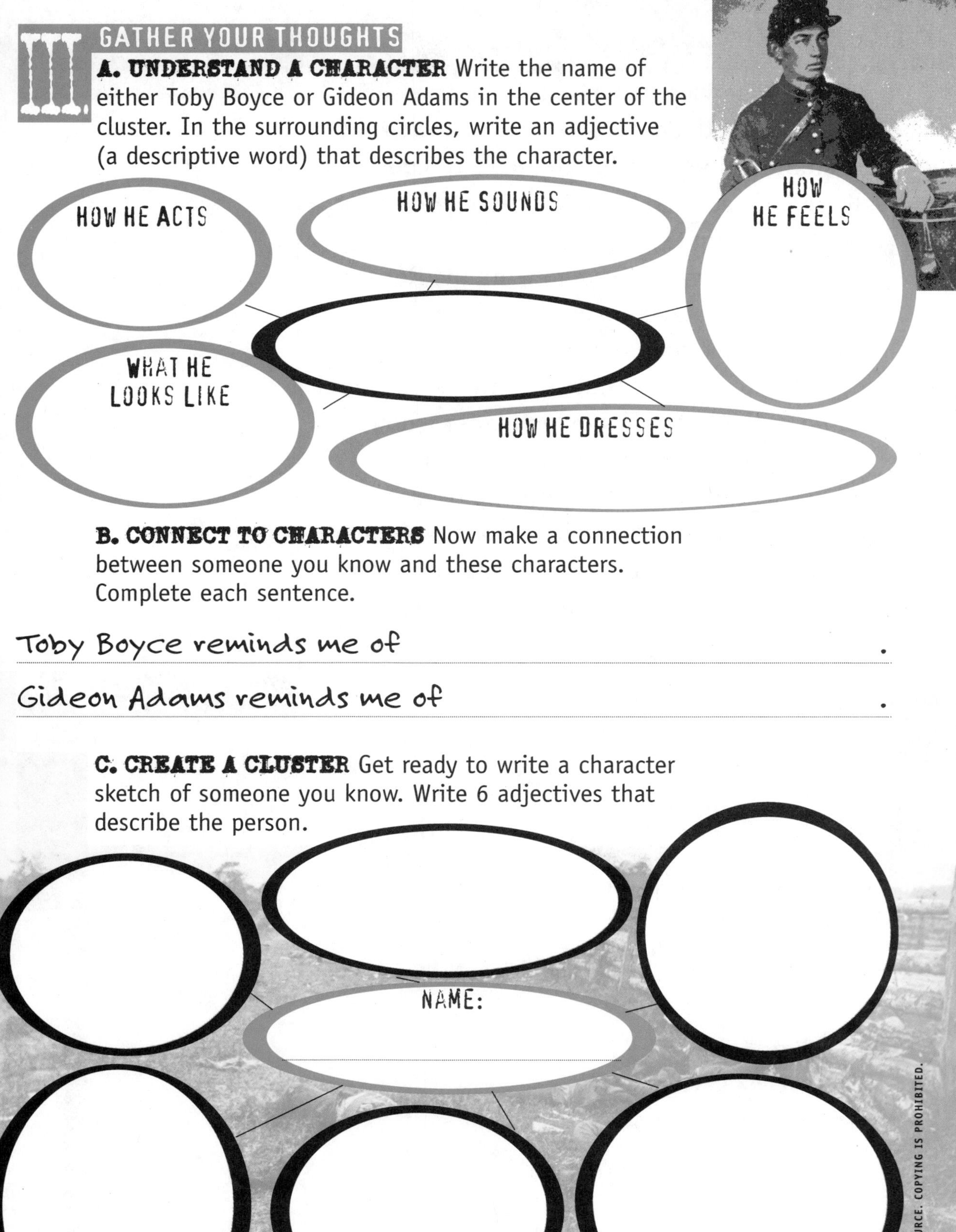

B. CONNECT TO CHARACTERS Now make a connection between someone you know and these characters. Complete each sentence.

Toby Boyce reminds me of ________________________.

Gideon Adams reminds me of ________________________.

C. CREATE A CLUSTER Get ready to write a character sketch of someone you know. Write 6 adjectives that describe the person.

NAME:

Now write a **character sketch** of the person you described in your web.

1. Begin with a topic sentence that explains who this person is.
2. Then give some details about him or her. Finish with a sentence that ties everything together.
3. Use the Writers' Checklist to help you revise.

WRITERS' CHECKLIST

CAPITALIZATION

- ❑ **Did you capitalize all proper nouns? A proper noun is a noun that names a specific person, place, or thing.** EXAMPLES: *Téa Rodriguez, Cobbles Elementary School, Corvette*
- ❑ **Did you capitalize the pronoun *I* (which refers to a specific person)?**

V. WRAP-UP

What did "Toby Boyce" and "Gideon Adams" make you think about?

READERS' CHECKLIST

DEPTH

- ❑ **Did the reading make you think about things?**
- ❑ **Did it set off thoughts beyond the surface topic?**

How important are first impressions? When you first see someone or something, you often form an impression almost instantly. You can do the same with your reading, too.

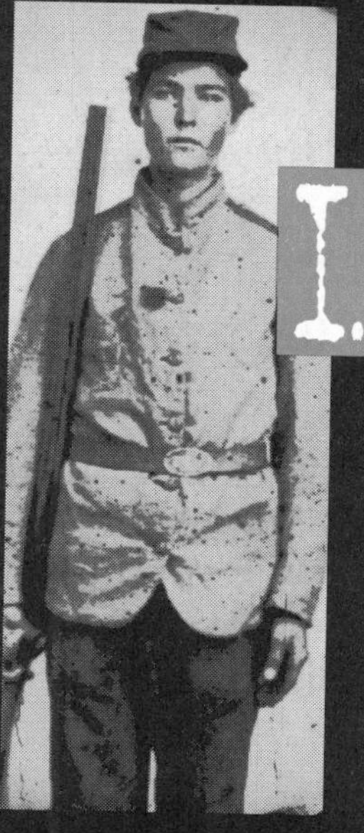

I. BEFORE YOU READ

One way to form an impression is to try to guess what a story is about based on a list of words taken from the story.

1. Look at the example Story Impression for "Shem Suggs" below.
2. Then complete the one for "Judah Jenkins." Read the words on the left. Make a guess about what the story is about. Then form your story by using each of the words in a sentence.

STORY IMPRESSION

"SHEM SUGGS"

civil wars
soldiers
order
bullets
frightful

During civil wars, both men and horses know the danger.

Every day soldiers died in battle.

The fighting destroyed all order among the troops.

The bullets and cannon fire were everywhere.

The war was frightful.

"JUDAH JENKINS"

retreat

forward

blood

roar

READ

Now read "Shem Suggs" and "Judah Jenkins."

1. As you read, underline the main events Fleischman describes.
2. **Clarify** what's happening by summarizing the main events in the Response Notes.

RESPONSE NOTES

EXAMPLE:
Soldiers stay awake.

"Shem Suggs" from *Bull Run* by Paul Fleischman

It was a warm night. We knew there'd soon be a battle. The horses knew it too. Greta was restless as a flea-bit dog, stamping her hooves and flicking her tail. Most of the company played at cards. No one seemed to want to turn in. One read a letter from his father saying war was uncivilized, low, immoral, and that civil wars were the worst of the brood. The letter was burned with great jollity. After a time, though, the men took to studying Bibles instead of poker hands. It struck me as strange that nearly all the legions of soldiers camped around me considered themselves to be whole-souled Christians, had heard preaching every Sunday of their lives, had memorized piles of Scripture verses, and yet were ready to break the commandment against killing the moment the order was given.

VOCABULARY

hooves—feet.
uncivilized—barbaric.
civil wars—wars between people of the same country.
worst of the brood—worst kind.
jollity—celebration.
legions—large numbers.

STOP AND RETELL

How does this story begin?

I went walking. I came to a man who was reading Gulliver's Travels to a circle of listeners. I stopped and gave ear. Gulliver had come to a curious country where horses ruled and men were thought to be the foulest of beasts. The horses, wise as they were, had no wars. They could scarcely believe it when Gulliver told them that soldiers were men paid to kill each other. Then he described sabers, muskets, bullets, cannons that left the field of battle strewn with bloody limbs, and other clever inventions that had led humans to think themselves far advanced beyond horses.

RESPONSE NOTES

STOP AND RETELL

What does Shem hear about Gulliver?

It was almost too frightful to laugh at. I dearly wished I might go to that land. When the man stopped reading, I promised myself that if I

VOCABULARY

Gulliver's Travels—Jonathan Swift's 1726 satiric novel about a man who travels to imaginary lands.
curious—unusual; odd.
sabers—swords with curved blades.
muskets—guns with long barrels.
strewn—scattered; covered.

RESPONSE NOTES

lived through the war I'd learn my letters and read the rest of that book. Then I visited with the horses a long spell, and tried not to think upon what was coming.

STOP AND RETELL

In your own words, what promise does Shem make to himself?

STOP AND RETELL

"Judah Jenkins" from *Bull Run* by Paul Fleischman

Since before first light I'd been standing about at General Beauregard's headquarters. Of a sudden, I was ordered to ride over to Colonel Evans, near the stone bridge, and bring back word on the Yanks' position. I'd been waiting to show my worth as a courier. I galloped toward the west. It dawned upon me that I was headed straight for the fighting. It dawned on my horse as well. The musket balls began to whiz past us. He slowed, two legs moving ahead while the other two tried to retreat.

VOCABULARY

General Beauregard's headquarters—the General's office of operations.
Yanks'—belonging to the Yankees, or Northern troops.
courier—messenger.
galloped—rode.
musket balls—bullets.

STOP AND RETELL

What problem is Judah having with his horse?

RESPONSE NOTES

I wrestled him forward, past soldiers waiting to advance. Others were firing in the woods. I spied Colonel Evans, hopped to the ground, and tied the reins tight to a tree. Just then I heard someone shout "Pull her off!" The next moment there came a tremendous roar. It was one of our cannons. A man who'd been standing too close to the muzzle was thrown twenty feet. Blood gushed out of one of his ears. I wondered if I wasn't deaf myself. Then I turned, saw the broken reins, and realized I was a courier whose horse had sprinted away.

STOP AND RETELL

How did Judah do at "showing his worth"?

VOCABULARY

muzzle—front of the gun barrel.

III. GATHER YOUR THOUGHTS

A. CONNECT WITH A CHARACTER Which character would you rather talk to, Shem Suggs or Judah Jenkins? Circle your choice. Write 2-3 reasons explaining your choice.

1.

2.

3.

B. BRAINSTORM Get together with a small group. Brainstorm a list of 5 questions you'd like to ask Shem or Judah. Write your questions here.

1.

2.

3.

4.

5.

C. CREATE DIALOGUE A dialogue is a conversation between 2 people or characters. Get ready to write a dialogue between either Shem or Judah and yourself.

1. Read the example question and answer below. Note the way the sentences are punctuated.
2. Then write another question and another answer.

EXAMPLE: **I asked, "Where are you from, Judah?"**

"I'm from a small place up north," Judah replied.

QUESTION

ANSWER

IV. WRITE

Now write a **dialogue** between yourself and either Shem or Judah.

1. Begin by asking the character a question.
2. Then write the character's response. Add 1–2 other questions or statements to your conversation.
3. Use the Writers' Checklist to help you revise.

WRITERS' CHECKLIST

DIALOGUE

- ❑ **Did you use quotation marks at the beginning and the end of each quotation?** EXAMPLE: ***"I was very scared," Shem said quietly.***
- ❑ **Did you use commas to separate quotations from speech tags?** EXAMPLE: ***"I was standing around at the general's headquarters," Judah explained.***
- ❑ **Did you check to see that the quotation itself contains the correct punctuation?** EXAMPLE: ***"Did you ever find your horse, Judah?" I asked nervously.***

V. WRAP-UP

What did you like most about Paul Fleischman's style of writing? What did you like least?

READERS' CHECKLIST

STYLE

- ❑ **Did you find the passage well written?**
- ❑ **Are the sentences well constructed and the words well chosen?**
- ❑ **Does the style show you how to be a better writer?**

Memories

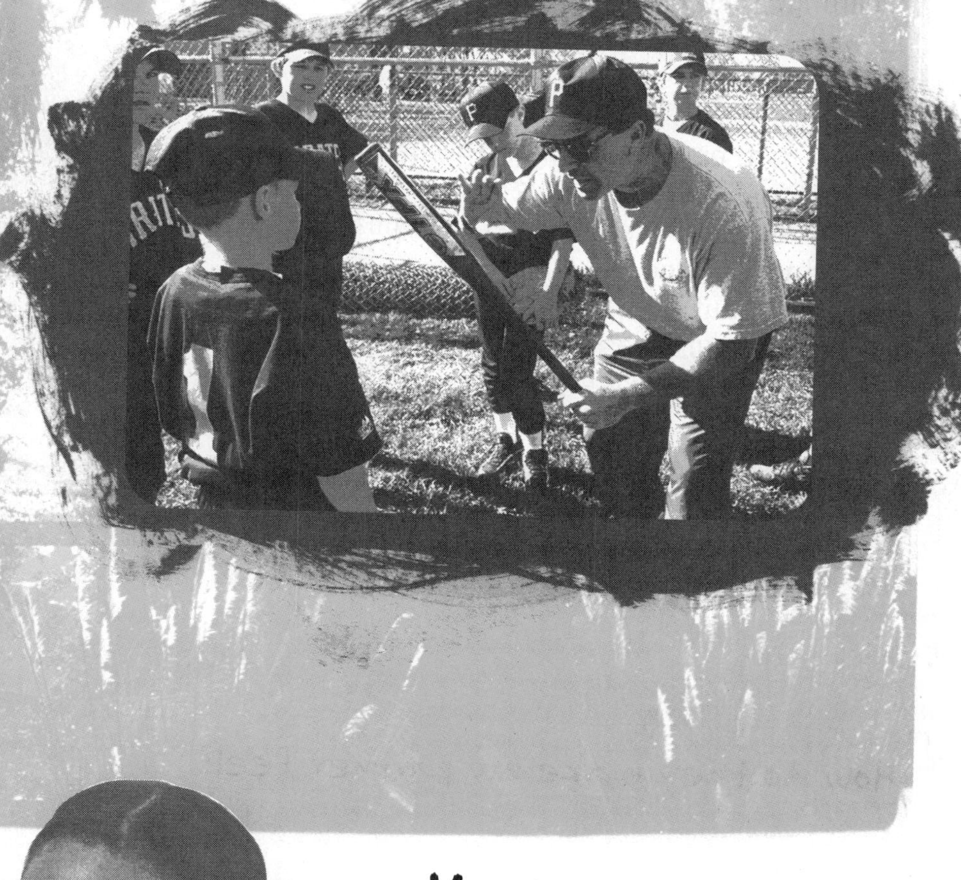

Memories can fade with time or become more vivid with each passing day. Memory is a powerful and precious gift that enables people to turn back the clock and relive private experiences of the past.

7: A Moment in the Sun Field

Getting ready to read is like getting ready to cross the railroad tracks. You need to stop, look, and listen. This is especially true when what you're reading has pictures. Before you read, take a picture walk. Stop at each picture. Look for clues about the story's meaning. Then listen to others' ideas about the story as well.

I. BEFORE YOU READ

With a partner, walk through the pictures in "A Moment in the Sun Field."

1. Look at each image. Pick 1 or 2 images that you find interesting.
2. Think about how they make you feel.
3. Discuss your ideas with your partner and answer the questions below.

Picture Walk

How do the images make me feel?

How do they make my partner feel?

What will this story be about?

What does my partner think the story will be about?

II. READ

Now read "A Moment in the Sun Field."

1. Think about how the story and its setting make you feel.
2. Make sketches to help you **visualize** the people and scene being described.

Response Notes

"A Moment in the Sun Field"
by William Brohaugh

Deep into the summer and not too long after Bobby Hansen's twelfth birthday, after one of Bobby's mom's hamburger suppers, Mike Pasqui came over to Bobby's house and the two of them talked Bobby's dad into playing some 500 with them. Dad grumbled a little—he always did—but he grabbed the bat and ball from the back porch and headed for the back yard with Mytzi, Bobby's muttzy dog, yapping behind—and he always did that, too.

EXAMPLE:

Mike and Bobby took the field first, and Dad hit balls to them. A caught fly ball earned Bobby 100 points. A grounder played on one bounce earned Mike 75. A flubbed grounder—a two-bouncer—stole 50 points back from Mike. And on it went into the evening. When one of the players earned 500 points, he took the bat until someone else got 500. Mike didn't do much batting, which was okay with him. He just liked being a part of the game. And since Dad preferred to bat, after a while he decided

VOCABULARY

playing some 500—game in which a batter hits a baseball and the fielder who catches it receives points for each catch, until someone reaches 500 points.
muttzy—mixed-bred.
flubbed—failed.

Double-entry Journal

Write your thoughts about the quote below.

Quote	My thoughts
"Dad grumbled a little—he always did—but he grabbed the bat and ball from the back porch. . . ."	

Response Notes

to do all the batting no matter who scored how many points. And that was okay with everyone, too.

Pretty soon, Bobby had 1,075 points, and Mike had around 300 (he had stopped counting), and Dad was swinging and smacking the ball and even joking around a little bit.

It wasn't too long and the shadow of the house slid up on Dad, slid over him, and stretched for the horizon, which it would reach, Bobby knew, the moment the sun disappeared below the opposite horizon. It would be a shadow hundreds of miles long, millions of miles long, and Bobby sometimes wondered if that was what night really was, all the

VOCABULARY

horizon—line along which the earth and sky appear to meet.
opposite horizon—other end of the sky.

"A Moment in the Sun Field" continued

Response Notes

shadows of all the houses and all the dads and all the kids playing 500 stretched out and added together.

Dad tossed the ball into the air in front of him and popped a fly out of the shadow and into the sunlight. The sun splashed onto one side of the ball, splashed it cool and white against the cool and darkening sky. The ball spun, and began to fall, and Bobby positioned himself under it, held his glove out not for a whole ball, but just a piece of one, because it looked like just a piece of one, a slice of ball, the slice splashed extra white in the high sunlight.

Bobby waited for that little bit of ball to come down, and suddenly he understood the moon.

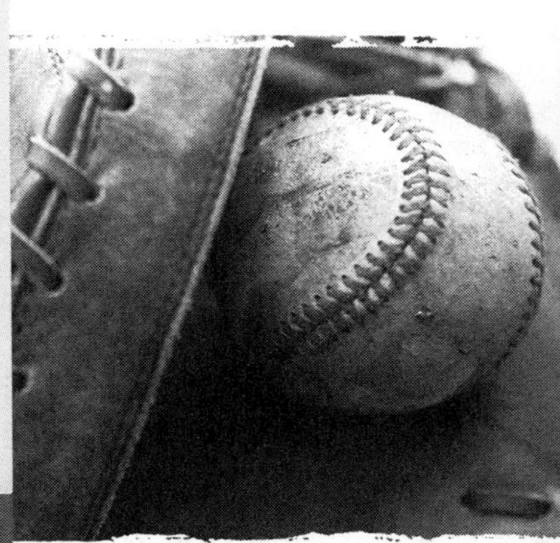

Double-entry Journal

In the right-hand column, write your response to the quotes below.

Quotes	My thoughts
1. "The sun splashed onto one side of the ball, splashed it cool and white against the cool and darkening sky."	
2. "Bobby waited for that little bit of ball to come down, and suddenly he understood the moon."	

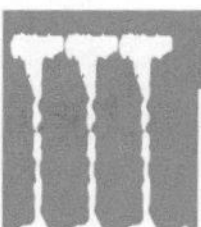

GATHER YOUR THOUGHTS

A. VISUALIZE A SCENE In the frame below, draw a sketch of Bobby's backyard. Use your imagination for the parts that Brohaugh does not describe.

B. USE DESCRIPTIVE WORDS Prepare to write a paragraph describing the setting of "A Moment in the Sun Field." Build a word bank of descriptive words.

1. Look back at the story. Find 3-4 descriptive words or phrases from the story.
2. Then write 3-4 words or phrases that you think describe the setting and scene you drew above.

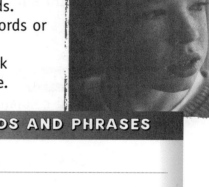

WORDS FROM THE STORY	MY WORDS AND PHRASES

IV. WRITE

Write a **descriptive paragraph** about the setting of "A Moment in the Sun Field."

1. Begin with a topic sentence that explains where and when the story takes place.
2. Then offer details about the setting, using the words from your word bank.
3. Use the Writers' Checklist to help you revise.

WRITERS' CHECKLIST

COMPOUND SENTENCES

❑ **Did you use commas and conjunctions, such as *and*, *or*, and *but* to separate the two parts of compound sentences? If you use a comma, but not also a conjunction, to separate the two parts, the result is a comma splice.**
EXAMPLE: *He is an excellent batter, but he needs work on fielding.*

V. WRAP-UP

What did "A Moment in the Sun Field" mean to you?

READERS' CHECKLIST

MEANING

❑ **Did you learn something from the reading?**
❑ **Did it affect you or make an impression?**

8: The One Sitting There

Can you feel more than 1 emotion at a time—maybe even 3 or 4 at once? The author of "The One Sitting There" thinks you can. It is a story about a woman who feels grief and relief and happiness and loss all at the same time.

I. BEFORE YOU READ

Read the statements below.

1. Mark whether you agree or disagree with each statement.
2. When you've finished reading "The One Sitting There," react to the statements again.

Anticipation Guide

BEFORE YOU READ agree	BEFORE YOU READ disagree		AFTER YOU READ agree	AFTER YOU READ disagree
		1. When someone you love dies, you feel guilty.		
		2. It's impossible to overcome the feelings of guilt when someone you love dies.		
		3. A parent who suffers the loss of a child suffers the worst loss of all.		
		4. Ordinary things can remind you of sad memories.		
		5. Sometimes you have to think about your own happiness.		
		6. People who think about their own happiness are usually selfish.		

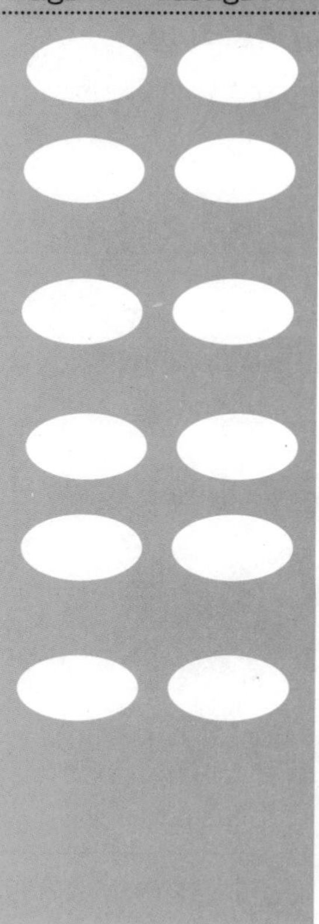

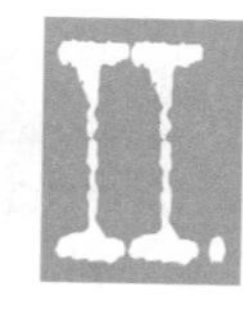

II. READ

Now read "The One Sitting There."

1. As you read, think about what you like and dislike about the story.
2. **React** to parts of the story by writing comments in the Response Notes.

Response Notes

"The One Sitting There" by Joanna H. Woś

I threw away the meat. The dollar ninety-eight a pound ground beef, the boneless chicken, the spareribs, the hamsteak. I threw the soggy vegetables into the trashcan: the carrots, broccoli, peas, the Brussels sprouts. I poured the milk down the drain of the stainless steel sink. The cheddar cheese I ground up in the disposal. The ice cream, now liquid, followed. All the groceries in the refrigerator had to be thrown away. The voice on the radio hinted of germs thriving on the food after the hours without power. Throwing the food away was rational and reasonable.

EXAMPLE:
slow plot—not much happening

stop+clarify

What's the narrator doing? Why?

....

....

....

stop+clarify

In our house, growing up, you were never allowed to throw food away. There was a

VOCABULARY

broccoli—green vegetable with flower buds.
Brussels sprouts—small vegetables that grow on a stalk.
disposal—electronic device below the sink that grinds garbage.
germs—bacteria; disease causing organisms.
rational—logical.

reason. My mother saved peelings and spoiled things to put on the compost heap. That would go back into the garden to grow more vegetables. You could leave meat or potatoes to be used again in soup. But you were never allowed to throw food away.

stop+predict

What do you predict is the reason for doing these things?

I threw the bread away. The bread had gotten wet. I once saw my father pick up a piece of Wonder Bread he had dropped on the ground. He brushed his hand over the slice to remove the dirt and then kissed the bread. Even at six I knew why he did that. My sister was the reason. I was born after the war. She lived in a time before. I do not know much about her. My mother never talked about her. There are no pictures. The only time my father talked about her was when he described how she clutched the bread so tightly in her baby fist that the bread squeezed out between her fingers. She sucked at the bread that way.

So I threw the bread away last. I threw the bread away for all the times I sat crying over a bowl of cabbage soup my father said I had to eat. Because eating would not bring her back. Because I would still be the one sitting there.

VOCABULARY

peelings—skins or rinds of fruit.
compost heap—pile of fertilizer made from decaying fruits and vegetables.
cabbage—vegetable with overlapping leaves.

"The One Sitting There" continued

Response Notes

Now I had the bread. I had gotten it. I had bought it. I had put it in the refrigerator. I had earned it. It was mine to throw away.

stop+question

What do you think happened to the narrator's sister?

So I threw the bread away for my sister. I threw the bread away and brought her back. She was twenty-one and had just come home from Christmas shopping. She had bought me a doll. She put the package on my dining room table and hung her coat smelling of perfume and the late fall air on the back of one of the chairs. I welcomed her as an honored guest. As if she were a Polish bride returning to her home, I greeted her with a plate of bread and salt. The bread, for prosperity, was wrapped in a white linen cloth. The salt, for tears, was in a small blue bowl. We sat down together and shared a piece of bread.

In a kitchen, where such an act was an ordinary thing, I threw away the bread. Because I could.

VOCABULARY

perfume—pleasing scent.
prosperity—success; good luck.

What is the theme of Woś's story?

Now return to your Anticipation Guide. Mark your answers in the "After You Read" column.

III. GATHER YOUR THOUGHTS

A. REACT TO A STORY What's your opinion of "The One Sitting There"? Use the scales below to rate the story. Circle the rating that you think is most appropriate.

THE PLOT IS . . .

1	2	3	4	5	6	7	8	9	10
not at all interesting				sort of interesting					very interesting

THE NARRATOR IS . . .

1	2	3	4	5	6	7	8	9	10
not easy to relate to				somewhat easy to relate to					very easy to relate to

THE SETTING IS . . .

1	2	3	4	5	6	7	8	9	10
not at all well-developed				fairly well-developed					very well-developed

THE MAIN IDEA IS . . .

1	2	3	4	5	6	7	8	9	10
not easy to understand				somewhat easy to understand					very easy to understand

B. SUPPORT AN OPINION Use your ratings to help you answer this question. List 3 facts or details that you could include in a review of "The One Sitting There."

Is "The One Sitting There" a good story?

yes **no** (circle one)

For these reasons:

1. ______________________________

2. ______________________________

3. ______________________________

It is never enough to just offer an opinion. You need to support your opinions.

IV. WRITE

Write a **review** of "The One Sitting There."

1. Start with a topic sentence that gives your overall opinion of the story.
2. Then support your opinion with facts and details from the story.
3. End with a closing sentence in which you explain whether you would recommend the story.
4. Use the Writers' Checklist to help you revise.

WRITERS' CHECKLIST

POSSESSIVES

Possessive nouns show ownership.

- ❑ **Did you add an 's to form the possessive of singular nouns?** EXAMPLES: *The one bee's hive, Mr. Jones's store*
- ❑ **Did you add an ' to form the possessive of plural nouns that end in *s*?** EXAMPLES: *the many bees' hive, the Joneses' store*
- ❑ **Did you add 's to form the possessive of plural nouns that do not end in *s*?** EXAMPLES: *the children's room, the mice's cheese*

V. WRAP-UP

What is the author's message in "The One Sitting There"?

READERS' CHECKLIST

UNDERSTANDING

- ❑ Did you understand the reading?
- ❑ Was the message or point clear?
- ❑ Can you restate what the reading is about?

Pandora

Hera

Mythology

From earliest times, people relied on myths to understand life's mysteries. Stories of gods, monsters, and heroes answered questions about the world and the role of human beings in it. The Greeks and Romans are especially famous for their myths, which have inspired masterworks of art around the world.

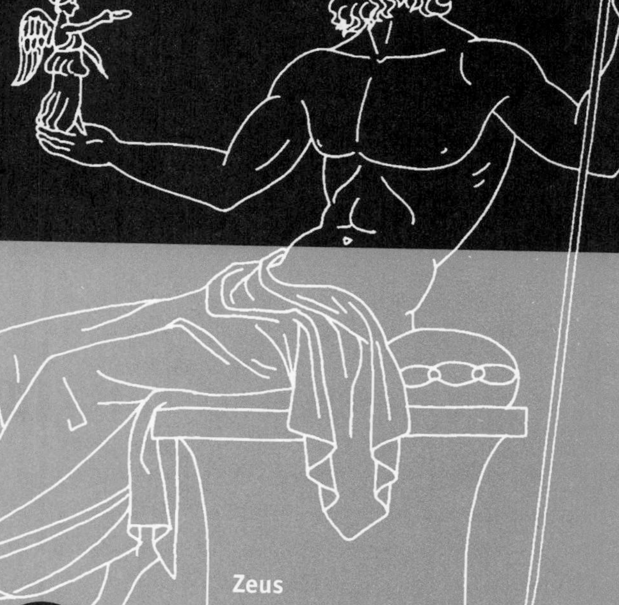
Zeus

Pandora

You may have heard the story of Pandora, the woman who opened a box that she wasn't supposed to. But what was inside the box, and who gave it to her? Previewing can help you find out answers to questions that are interesting or important.

BEFORE YOU READ

In a preview, you look for names and places, repeated words, key events, and unfamiliar vocabulary words.

1. Read the title and first paragraph of "Pandora." Then look at the questions on the Preview Card.
2. Glance quickly through the rest of the story. Look for information to answer the questions.

"Pandora" by Bernard Evslin

After Zeus had condemned Prometheus to his long torment for having given man fire, he began to plan how to punish man for having accepted it.

VOCABULARY

Prometheus—(Pro-MEE thi us) in Greek mythology, a giant who stole fire from the gods. As punishment, Zeus chained him to a rock.

torment—suffering.

WHAT ARE SOME KEY NAMES AND PLACES?	WHAT REPEATED WORDS DID YOU FIND?

WHAT ARE SOME KEY EVENTS?	WHAT UNFAMILIAR VOCABULARY WORDS DID YOU SEE?

II. READ

Now read the rest of "Pandora" with a partner.

1. Write any **questions** you have about the plot in the Response Notes.
2. Discuss your guesses about what will happen next. If you and your partner make different predictions, try to figure out why.

"Pandora" continued

Finally, he hit upon a scheme. He ordered Hephaestus to mold a girl out of clay, and to have Aphrodite pose for it to make sure it was beautiful. He breathed life into the clay figure, the clay turned to flesh, and she lay sleeping, all new. Then he summoned the gods, and asked them each to give her a gift.

Apollo taught her to sing, Demeter to tend a garden. Aphrodite taught her how to look at a man without moving her eyes, and how to dance without moving her legs. Poseidon gave her a pearl necklace and promised she would never drown. And, finally, Hermes gave her a beautiful golden box, which, he told her, she must never, never open. And then Hera gave her curiosity.

RESPONSE NOTES

EXAMPLE:
How will this clay woman be a punishment for mankind?

STOP AND PREDICT

What will the gods do with Pandora now?

Hermes took her by the hand and led her down the slope of Olympus. He led her to

VOCABULARY

scheme—clever plan.
Hephaestus—(Hi FESS tuss) in Greek mythology, the physically disabled god of metal-working and craftsmanship.
Aphrodite—(Af roe DIE tee) in Greek mythology, the beautiful goddess of love.
Hermes—(HER meez) in Greek mythology, the messenger of the gods.
curiosity—a desire to know or learn.

RESPONSE NOTES

Epimetheus, brother of Prometheus, and said, "Father Zeus grieves at the disgrace which has fallen upon your family. And to show you that he holds you blameless in your brother's offense, he makes you this gift—this girl, fairest in all the world. She is to be your wife. Her name is Pandora, the all-gifted."

So Epimetheus and Pandora were married. Pandora spun and baked and tended her garden, and played the lyre and danced for her husband, and thought herself the happiest young bride in all the world. Only one thing bothered her—the golden box. First she kept it on the table and polished it every day so that all might admire it. But the sunlight lanced through the window, and the box sparkled and seemed to be winking at her.

She found herself thinking, "Hermes must have been teasing. He's always making jokes; everyone knows that. Yes, he was teasing, telling me never to open his gift. For if it is so beautiful outside, what must it be inside? Truly, he has hidden a surprise for me there. Gems more lovely than have ever been seen, no doubt. If the box is so rich, the gift inside must be even more fine—for that is the way of gifts. Perhaps Hermes is *waiting* for me to open the box and see what is inside, and be

VOCABULARY

Epimetheus—(Ep ih ME thoos) in Greek mythology, Prometheus's brother and Pandora's husband.
grieves—feels sadness.
lyre—musical instrument with strings.

"Pandora" continued

delighted, and thank him. Perhaps he thinks me ungrateful. . . ."

RESPONSE NOTES

STOP AND PREDICT

What do you think is inside the box?

But even as she was telling herself this, she knew it was not so—that the box must not be opened—that she must keep her promise.

Finally, she took the box from the table, and hid it in a dusty little storeroom. But it seemed to be burning there in the shadows. Its heat seemed to scorch her thoughts wherever she went. She kept passing that room, and stepping into it, making excuses to dawdle there. Sometimes she took the box from its hiding place and stroked it, then quickly shoved it out of sight, and rushed out of the room.

She took it then, locked it in a heavy oaken chest, put great shackles on the chest, and dug a hole in her garden. She put the chest in, covered it over, and rolled a boulder on top of it. When Epimetheus came home that night, her hair was wild and her hands were bloody, her tunic torn and stained. But all she would

VOCABULARY

scorch—burn.
dawdle—hang around.
shackles—metal locks.
boulder—large rock.
tunic—loose-fitting outfit.

RESPONSE NOTES

tell him was that she had been working in the garden.

STOP AND PREDICT

Do you predict Epimetheus will try to stop Pandora from opening the box?

That night the moonlight blazed into the room. She could not sleep. The light pressed her eyes open. She sat up in the bed and looked around. All the room was swimming in moonlight. Everything was different. There were deep shadows and swaths of silver, all mixed, all moving. She arose quietly and tiptoed from the room.

She went out into the garden. The flowers were blowing, the trees were swaying. The whole world was adance in the magic white fire of that moonlight. She walked to the rock and pushed it. It rolled away as lightly as a pebble. And she felt herself full of wild strength.

She took a shovel and dug down to the chest. She unshackled it, and drew out the golden box. It was cold, cold; coldness burned her hand to the bone. She trembled. What was inside that box seemed to know the very secret of life, which she must look upon or die.

VOCABULARY

swaths—strips.
adance—ablaze; lighted up.

RESPONSE NOTES

She took the little golden key from her tunic, fitted it into the keyhole, and gently opened the lid. There was a swarming, a hot throbbing, a wild meaty rustling, and a foul smell. Out of the box, as she held it up in the moonlight, swarmed small scaly lizardlike creatures with bat wings and burning red eyes.

They flew out of the box, circled her head once, clapping their wings and screaming thin little jeering screams—and then flew off into the night, hissing and cackling.

STOP AND PREDICT

What do you think Pandora will do next? Explain.

Then, half-fainting, sinking to her knees, Pandora, with her last bit of strength, clutched the box and slammed down the lid—catching the last little monster just as it was wriggling free. It shrieked and spat and clawed her hand, but she thrust it back into the box and locked it in. Then she dropped the box, and fainted away.

What were those deathly creatures that flew out of the golden box? They were the ills

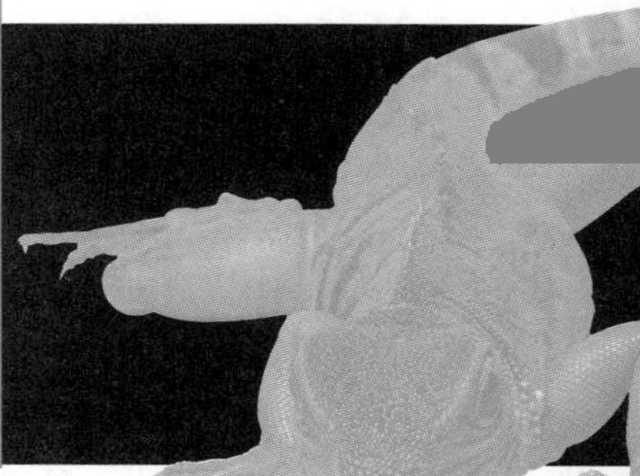

VOCABULARY

rustling—soft sound.
scaly—flaky.
jeering—mocking; sarcastic.
hissing and cackling—making high pitched, loud sounds.
shrieked—screamed.
spat—spit.

RESPONSE NOTES

that beset mankind: the spites, disease in its thousand shapes, old age, famine, insanity, and all their foul kin. After they flew out of the box they scattered—flew into every home, and swung from the rafters—waiting. And when their time comes they fly and sting—and bring pain and sorrow and death.

At that, things could have been much worse. For the creature that Pandora shut into the box was the most dangerous of all. It was foreboding, the final spite. If it had flown free, everyone in the world would have been told exactly what misfortune was to happen every day of his life. No hope would have been possible. And so there would have been an end to man. For, though he can bear endless trouble, he cannot live with no hope at all.

VOCABULARY

beset—troubled.
famine—starvation.
insanity—craziness; mental illness.
foul kin—obnoxious relatives.
rafters—beams that support the roof.
foreboding—a sign of coming evil.

STOP AND REFLECT STOP AND REFLECT STOP AND REFLECT

Think back over the predictions you made about the events in "Pandora."

How accurate were your predictions overall? Why?

III. GATHER YOUR THOUGHTS

A. RECALL THE PLOT Use this storyboard to show the 6 main events in the plot of "Pandora." What happens first? What happens next? Draw a picture and write a brief caption in each frame.

1.

2.

3.

4.

5.

6.

B. CONTINUE THE PLOT Recall what happens at the end of "Pandora." Pandora has fainted, and the evil creatures have flown away. Think about what happens when Pandora wakes up again. Brainstorm ideas about what she might do, where she might go, and how she might feel.

WHAT PANDORA MIGHT DO . . .	WHERE PANDORA MIGHT GO . . .	HOW PANDORA MIGHT FEEL . . .

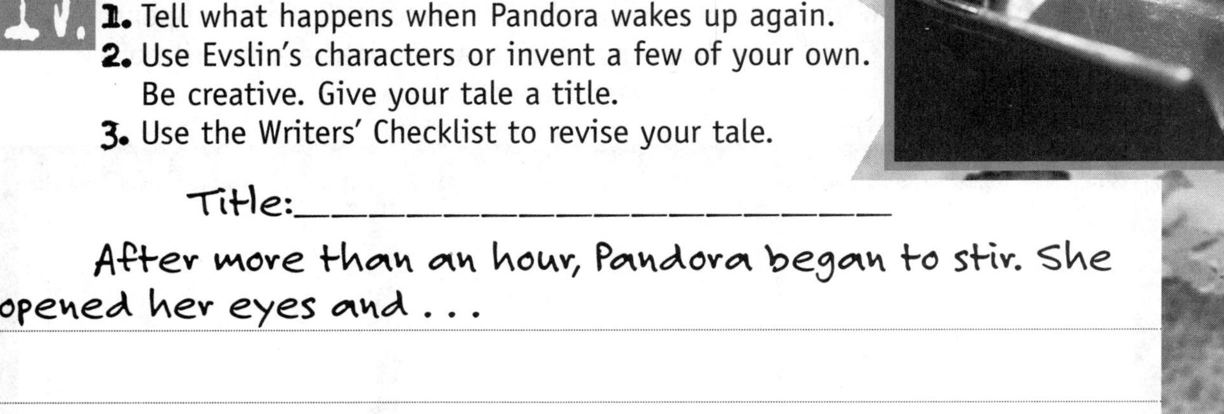

IV. WRITE

Write a **tale** that continues the story of Pandora.

1. Tell what happens when Pandora wakes up again.
2. Use Evslin's characters or invent a few of your own. Be creative. Give your tale a title.
3. Use the Writers' Checklist to revise your tale.

Title: ________________________

After more than an hour, Pandora began to stir. She opened her eyes and . . .

WRITERS' CHECKLIST

VERBS

❑ Did you avoid mixing verb tenses? Present tense verbs show action that is happening now: *sleep*, *eat*, *look*. Past tense verbs show action that has happened in the past: *slept*, *ate*, *looked*. Mixing verb tenses can confuse a reader about what happens when.

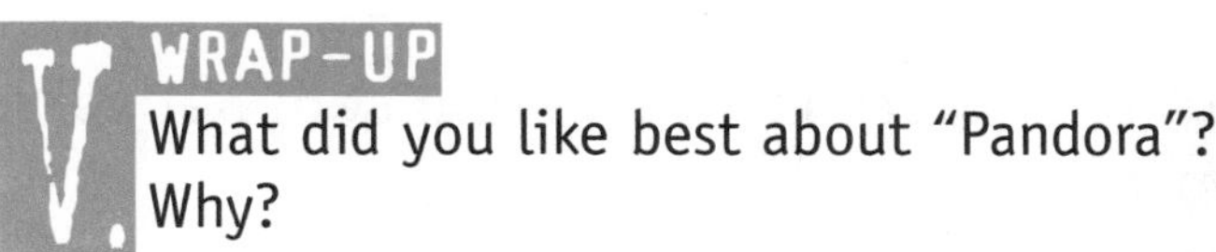

V. WRAP-UP

What did you like best about "Pandora"? Why?

READERS' CHECKLIST

ENJOYMENT

❑ Did you like the reading?

❑ Was the reading experience pleasurable?

❑ Would you want to reread the piece or recommend it to someone?

Do you like stories about powerful characters, plans for revenge, and fierce beasts? If so, you'll love the plots and characters of famous myths. Hera was probably the most powerful goddess in all of Greek mythology, and she took great pleasure in causing trouble for mortals and immortals alike.

I. BEFORE YOU READ

THINK-PAIR-SHARE

Pair up with one or more reading partners.

1. Take turns reading aloud these sentences from "Hera."
2. Number which sentence appears first, which second, and so on.
3. Then answer the questions below.

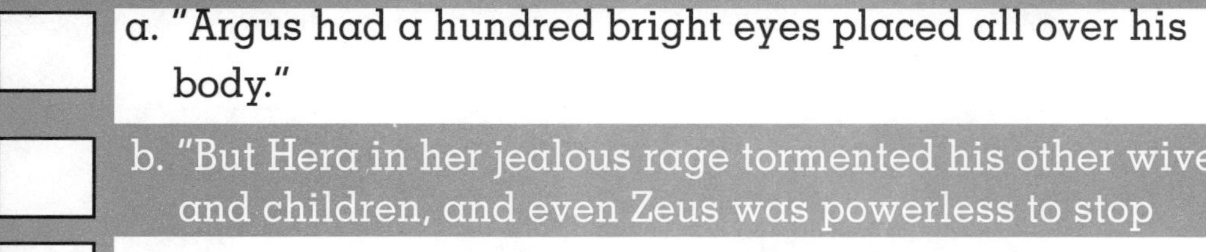

☐ a. "Argus had a hundred bright eyes placed all over his body."

☐ b. "But Hera in her jealous rage tormented his other wives and children, and even Zeus was powerless to stop

☐ c. "Hera tied poor Io to a tree and sent her servant Argus to keep watch over her."

☐ d. "Slyly Zeus created a thunderstorm, changed himself into a little cuckoo, and, pretending to be in distress, he flew into Hera's arms for protection."

What did you learn about Hera from reading these sentences?

What did you learn about Zeus?

II. READ

Now read "Hera."

1. As you read, **mark** or **highlight** important information about characters.
2. Jot comments in the Response Notes about characters' important actions or personality traits.

"Hera" by Ingri and Edgar Parin d'Aulaire

RESPONSE NOTES

EXAMPLE: Hera = strong emotions and stubborn

Hera, the beautiful queen of Olympus, was a very jealous wife. Even Zeus, who was afraid of nothing, feared her fits of temper. She hated all his other wives, and when Zeus first asked her to be his wife, she refused. Slyly Zeus created a thunderstorm, changed himself into a little cuckoo, and, pretending to be in distress, he flew into Hera's arms for protection. She pitied the wet little bird and hugged it close to keep it warm, but all of a sudden she found herself holding mighty Zeus in her arms instead of the bird.

Thus Zeus won Hera and all nature burst into bloom for their wedding. Mother Earth gave the bride a little apple tree that bore golden apples of immortality. Hera treasured the tree and planted it in the garden of the Hesperides, her secret garden far to the west. She put a hundred-headed dragon under the tree to guard the apples and ordered the three Nymphs of the Hesperides to water and care for the tree.

Zeus loved Hera dearly, but he was also very fond of rocky Greece. He often sneaked

VOCABULARY

cuckoo—bird.
distress—pain.
immortality—never ending life.
Hesperides—(Hess PER i deez) in Greek mythology, the group of nymphs who watch over Hera's garden.

RESPONSE NOTES

down to earth in disguise to marry mortal girls. The more wives he had, the more children he would have, and all the better for Greece! All his children would inherit some of his greatness and become great heroes and rulers. But Hera in her jealous rage tormented his other wives and children, and even Zeus was powerless to stop her. She knew how tricky Zeus could be and kept very close watch over him.

One day as Hera looked down on earth, she spied a small dark thundercloud where no cloud should have been. She rushed down and darted into the cloud. Zeus was there just as she had suspected, but with him was only a little snow-white cow. He had seen Hera coming and, to protect his newest bride Io from her wrath, he had changed the girl into a cow. Alas! The cow was as lovely as the girl, and Hera was not deceived, but she pretended to suspect nothing and begged Zeus to let her have the dainty cow. Zeus could not well refuse his queen such a little wish without giving himself away, and he had to give her the cow. Hera tied poor Io to a tree and sent her servant Argus to keep watch over her.

Argus had a hundred bright eyes placed all over his body. He was so big and strong that singlehandedly he had made an end to the

VOCABULARY

mortal—human.
inherit—receive.
tormented—greatly bothered; harassed.
wrath—rage; anger.
deceived—tricked; fooled.
dainty—delicate.

RESPONSE NOTES

monstrous Echidna, who had lived in a cave and had devoured all who passed by. He was Hera's faithful servant and the best of watchmen, for he never closed more than half of his eyes in sleep at a time.

Argus sat down next to the cow and watched her with all his eyes, and poor Io had to walk on four legs and eat grass. She raised her mournful eyes to Olympus, but Zeus was so afraid of Hera that he did not dare to help her. At last he could no longer bear to see her distress, and he asked his son Hermes, the craftiest of the gods, to run down to earth and set Io free.

STOP AND ORGANIZE

Use this graphic to organize what you know about Zeus.

Zeus

TRAIT

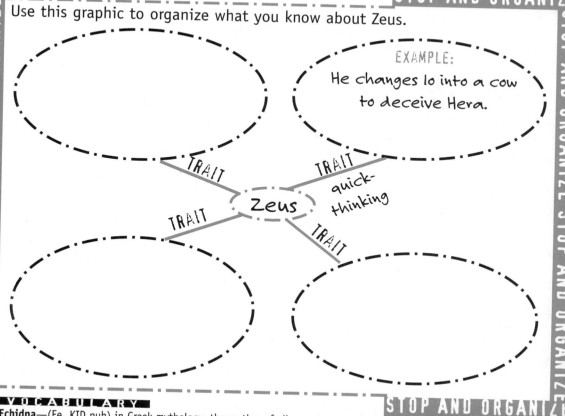

TRAIT quick-thinking

EXAMPLE: He changes Io into a cow to deceive Hera.

TRAIT

TRAIT

VOCABULARY

Echidna—(Ee KID nuh) in Greek mythology, the mother of all monsters.
mournful—sad.
craftiest—most clever.

RESPONSE NOTES

Hermes disguised himself as a shepherd and walked up to Argus playing a tune on his shepherd's pipe. Argus was bored, having nothing to do with all his eyes but watch a little cow, and he was glad to have music and company. Hermes sat down beside him, and after he had played for a while, he began to tell a long and dull story. It had no beginning and it had no end and fifty of Argus's eyes closed in sleep. Hermes droned on and on and slowly the fifty other eyes fell shut, one by one. Quickly Hermes touched all the eyes with his magic wand and closed them forever in eternal sleep. Argus had been bored to death.

Hermes then untied the cow, and Io ran home to her father, the river-god Inachos. He did not recognize the cow as his daughter, and Io could not tell him what had happened, all she could say was, "Mooo!" But when she lifted up her little hoof and scratched her name, "I-O," in the river sand, her father at once understood what had happened, for he knew the ways of Zeus. Inachos rose out of his river bed and rushed off to take revenge on the mighty thunder-god. He flew at Zeus in such a rage that to save himself Zeus had to throw a thunderbolt, and ever since the bed of the river Inachos in Arcadia has been dry.

Hera was furious when she saw that Argus was dead and the cow Io had been set free.

VOCABULARY

shepherd—person who takes care of sheep.
droned—spoke in a boring tone.
Inachos—(In AH kos) in Greek mythology, the river god and father of Io.

RESPONSE NOTES

She sent a vicious gadfly to sting and chase the cow. To be sure that her faithful servant Argus would never be forgotten, she took his hundred bright eyes and put them on the tail of the peacock, her favorite bird. The eyes could no longer see, but they looked gorgeous, and that went to the peacock's little head, and made it the vainest of all animals.

Pursued by the gadfly, Io ran all over Greece. Trying to escape from its tormenting sting, she jumped across the strait that separates Europe from Asia Minor, and, ever since, it has been called the Bosporus, the "cow ford."

But still the gadfly chased her all the way to the land of Egypt. When the Egyptians saw the snow-white cow, they fell to their knees and worshipped her. She became an Egyptian goddess, and Hera now permitted Zeus to change her back to her human shape. But first he had to promise never to look at Io again.

VOCABULARY

vicious gadfly—evil and annoying fly.
peacock—brightly colored, long-feathered bird with eyelike spots.
gorgeous—very beautiful.
strait—narrow channel joining two larger bodies of water.
Bosporus—narrow strait separating European and Asian Turkey. It is still an important trade route.

STOP AND ORGANIZE

Use this graphic to organize what you know about Hera.

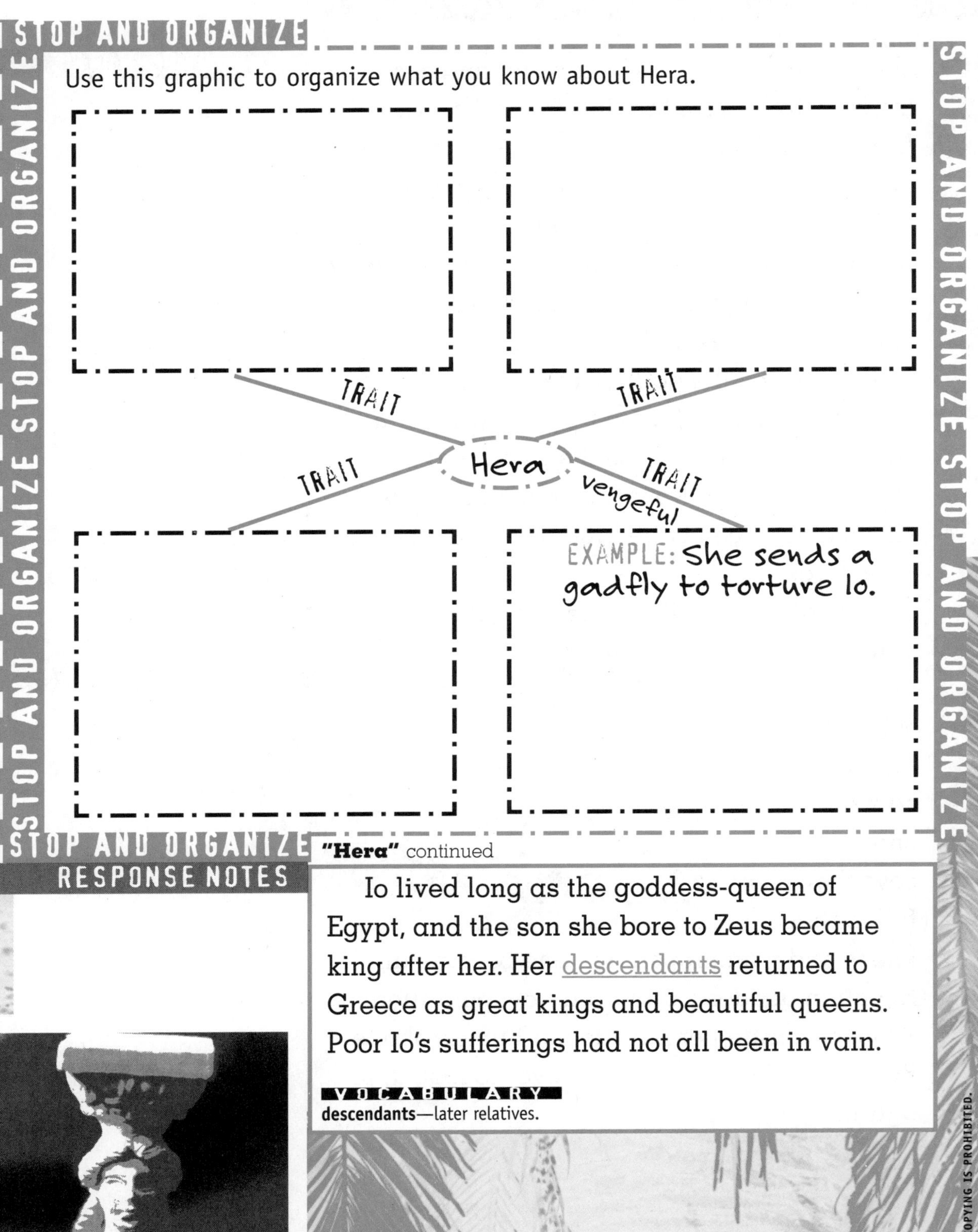

RESPONSE NOTES

"Hera" continued

Io lived long as the goddess-queen of Egypt, and the son she bore to Zeus became king after her. Her descendants returned to Greece as great kings and beautiful queens. Poor Io's sufferings had not all been in vain.

VOCABULARY

descendants—later relatives.

III. GATHER YOUR THOUGHTS

A. CLUSTER What words would you use to describe Zeus and Hera? Write words that show the various sides of each personality.

B. ORGANIZE DETAILS Get ready to write a description of either Zeus or Hera. Use the organizer below to arrange your information.

HOW THE CHARACTER LOOKS

HOW I FEEL ABOUT THE CHARACTER

CHARACTER NAME

HOW THE CHARACTER ACTS

HOW OTHER CHARACTERS FEEL ABOUT THE CHARACTER

Write a sentence that summarizes your character.

IV. WRITE

Now write a **descriptive paragraph** about Hera or Zeus.

1. Begin with a topic sentence that says what you think the character is really like. Use details from your organizer to support your topic sentence.
2. Use the Writers' Checklist to help you revise.

WRITERS' CHECKLIST

SUBJECT-VERB AGREEMENT

The subject and verb of a sentence must work together, or *agree*. A singular subject needs a singular verb. EXAMPLE: *Hera watches Io (not Hera watch Io).* **A plural subject needs a plural verb.** EXAMPLE: *Hera and Io were sworn enemies (not Hera and Io was sworn enemies).*

- ❑ **Did you always use singular verbs with singular subjects?**
- ❑ **Did you always use plural verbs with plural subjects?**

V. WRAP-UP

Did you find "Hera" easy or difficult to read? Explain why.

READERS' CHECKLIST

EASE

- ❑ **Was the passage easy to read?**
- ❑ **Were you able to read it smoothly and without difficulty?**

John Christopher

Born in 1922, Samuel Youd has published more than 70 novels under 7 different names. He has enjoyed the most success as John Christopher, an author of science-fiction novels and children's adventure stories. His most famous work is the *Tripods* trilogy. It was made into a film for British television.

How can you get at all the information that's buried deep inside you? One way is to ask yourself, "What do I already know about this topic?"

I. BEFORE YOU READ

"Arrival" is the beginning of a science-fiction novel. What do you already know about science fiction?

1. Create a web that explores what you know.
2. On the lines jutting outward from the center, write down words, phrases, and images that come to mind when you think of science fiction.
3. Share your web with the rest of the class. What can you learn from your classmates' webs?

science fiction

outer space

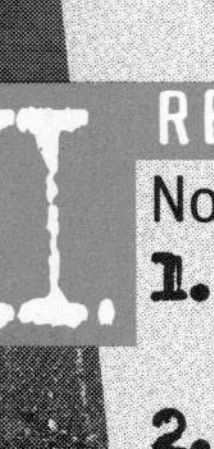

II. READ

Now read "Arrival."

1. As you read, think about the characters and how they react to what happens.
2. In the Response Notes, **clarify** your ideas about the characters.

"**Arrival**" from *When the Tripods Came* by John Christopher

RESPONSE NOTES

An explosion of noise woke me. It sounded as if a dozen express trains were about to hit the shed. I rolled over in my blanket trying to get out of the way, and was aware of a blaze of orange, lighting up boxes and bits of old farm equipment and tackle. An ancient rusting tractor looked briefly like an overgrown insect.

"What was that, Laurie?" Andy asked. I could see him sitting up, between me and the window.

"I don't know."

Both light and sound faded and died. A dog started barking—deep-throated, a Labrador maybe. I got up and walked to the window, banging my shin on something in the dark. It was dark outside, too, moon and stars hidden by cloud. A light came into the farmhouse, which was a couple of hundred meters away, just below the ridge.

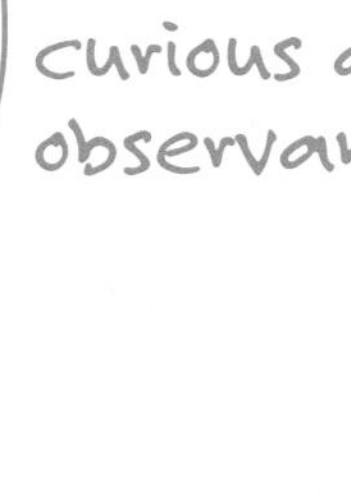
EXAMPLE:
Laurie is curious and observant.

I said, "It's not raining. What *was* it?"

"Didn't someone at the camp say something about an artillery range on the moor?"

VOCABULARY

tackle—rope.
ancient—very old.
tractor—vehicle with big tires used in mowing and farming.
moor—broad area of open land.

RESPONSE NOTES

"Nowhere near there, though."

"Whatever they were firing could have gone astray."

Rubbing my shin I said, "It didn't sound like a shell. And a shell wouldn't produce fireworks like that."

STOP AND PREDICT

What do you think is making the noise?

"A rocket, maybe." He yawned loudly. "It's all quiet now, anyway. No sweat. Go to sleep. We've a long trek in the morning."

I stood by the window for a while. Eventually the light in the house went out: the farmer presumably took the same view as Andy. In the pitch black I felt my way to the pile of straw which served as a bed. This was less fun than it had seemed the previous evening; there was little protection from the hardness of the earth floor, and once awake I knew all about the aches in my muscles,

Andy was already asleep. I blamed him for our being here—for volunteering us into the orienteering expedition in the first place, and then for insisting on a left fork which had taken us miles out of our way. It had looked as though we would have to spend the night on the moor,

VOCABULARY

shin—front part of the leg below the knee.
volunteering—offering.
orienteering expedition—training journey; exploration.

but we'd come across this isolated farm as dusk was thickening. The rules were not to ask for help, so we'd settled down in the shed.

I thought my aches, and resenting Andy, would keep me awake, but I was dead tired. We had set out early from summer camp, and it had been a long day's slog. Drifting into sleep again, I was half aware of another explosion, but it was a distant one, and I was too weary really to wake up—I couldn't even be sure I wasn't dreaming.

Andy woke me with the gray light of dawn filtering in. He said, "Listen."

"What?"

"Listen!"

I struggled into wakefulness. The noise was coming from the direction of the farmhouse, but further away, a succession of loud thumpings, heavy and mechanical.

"Farm machinery?" I suggested.

"I don't think so."

Listening more carefully, I didn't either. The thumps came at intervals of a second or less, and they were getting nearer. There was even a sensation of the ground shaking under me.

"Something heading this way," Andy said. "Something big, by the sound of it."

RESPONSE NOTES

VOCABULARY

dusk—darkness; twilight time.
slog—difficult walk.
thumpings—noises.
mechanical—machine-like.
intervals—time periods.
sensation—feeling.

RESPONSE NOTES

We crowded together at the small window of the shed. The sun hadn't risen, but to the east the farmhouse was outlined against a pearly sky. Smoke from a chimney rose almost straight: farmers were early risers. It looked like a good day for the trek back to camp. Then I saw what was coming into view on the other side of the house.

STOP AND PREDICT

What do you think is coming into view?

The top appeared first, an enormous gray-green hemispherical capsule, flat side down, which seemed to be floating ponderously in midair. But it wasn't floating: a weird stiltlike leg moved in a vast arc across the sky and planted itself just to the right of the farmhouse. As it crashed down, a second leg appeared, passing over the house and landing between it and the shed. I could see a third leg, too, which if it followed suit would come to ground close to us, if not on top of us. But at that point, it stopped. The gigantic object, more than twenty meters high, stood straddling the house.

VOCABULARY

pearly—bright.
trek—trip.
hemispherical capsule—round space object.
ponderously in midair—as though deep in thought and wondering what to do.
stiltlike—similar to a stilt or a long pole.
followed suit—did the same thing.
gigantic—huge.
straddling—with its legs on each side of.

RESPONSE NOTES

A band of bright green glassy panels ran horizontally along the side of the capsule. It produced an effect that was a cross between multiple staring eyes and a grinning mouth. It wasn't a pleasant grin.

"Someone's making a film." Andy's voice was unsteady. I turned to him and he looked as scared as I felt, "That must be it. A science-fiction movie."

"So where are the cameras?" I felt my voice was coming out wrong, too.

"They probably have to get it into position first."

I didn't know whether he believed it. I didn't.

Something was moving beneath the capsule, curling and twisting, and stretching out. It was like an elephant's trunk, or a snake, except that it was silvery and metallic. It corkscrewed down towards the roof of the house and brushed lightly against it. Then it moved to the chimney stack and grasped it with a curling tip. Bricks sprayed like confetti, and we heard them crashing onto the slates.

I was shivering. Inside the house a woman screamed. A door at the back burst open, and a man in shirt and trousers came out. He stared up at the machine looming above him and started running. Immediately a second tentacle uncurled, this time fast and purposeful. The tip

VOCABULARY

horizontally—parallel.
metallic—made from metal.
corkscrewed—twisted in a spiral.
confetti—small pieces of colored paper.
trousers—pants.
tentacle—long, flexible arm.

RESPONSE NOTES

caught him before he'd gone ten meters, fastened round his waist, and plucked him from the ground. He was screaming, too, now.

The tentacle lifted him up in front of the row of panels, and his screams turned to muffled groaning. After a few moments the tentacle twisted back on itself. A lenslike opening appeared at the base of the capsule; it carried him towards it and thrust him through. I thought of someone holding a morsel of food on a fork before popping it into his mouth, and felt sick.

His groans ended as the tentacle withdrew, and the opening closed. The woman in the house had also become quiet; but the silence was even more frightening. Resting on its spindly legs, the machine had the look of an insect digesting its prey. I remembered my glimpse of the derelict tractor in the night; this insect was as tall as King Kong.

STOP AND PREDICT

What will the machine do next?

....

....

....

For what seemed a long time, nothing happened. The thing didn't stir, and there was no sound or movement from the house. All was

VOCABULARY

fastened—attached; clung.
lenslike—similar to a lens or a glass.
morsel—small piece.
digesting—process that breaks down food after it has been eaten.
derelict tractor—abandoned farm vehicle used for plowing.

RESPONSE NOTES

still, not even a bird chirped. The tentacle hovered in midair, motionless and rigid.

When, after a minute or so, the tentacle did move, it raised itself higher, as though making a salute. For a second or two it hung in the air, before slamming down violently against the roof. Slates scattered, and rafters showed through a gaping hole. The woman started to shriek again.

Methodically the tentacle smashed the house, and as methodically picked over the ruins, like a scavenger going through a garbage can. The shrieking stopped, leaving just the din of demolition. A second tentacle set to work alongside the first, and a third joined them.

They probed deep into the rubble, lifting things up to the level of the panels. Most of what was picked up was dropped or tossed aside—chairs, a sideboard, a double bed, a bathtub dangling the metal pipes from which it had been ripped. A few were taken inside: I noticed an electric kettle and a television set.

At last it was over, and dust settled as the tentacles retracted under the capsule.

"I think we ought to get away from here," Andy said, his voice was so low I could hardly hear him.

"How far do you think it can see?"

"I don't know. But if we dodge out quickly, and get round the back . . ."

VOCABULARY

Slates—parts of the roof.
rafters—beams that support the roof.
ruins—mess.
scavenger—person who looks for food.
demolition—destruction.
rubble—destroyed pieces of rock.

RESPONSE NOTES

I gripped his arm. Something was moving at the base of the rubble that had been the farmhouse: a black dog wriggled free and started running across the farmyard. It covered about ten meters before a tentacle arrowed towards it. The dog was lifted, howling, in front of the panels, and held there. I thought it was going to be taken inside, as the man had been; instead the tentacle flicked it away. Briefly the dog was a black blur against the dawn light, then a crumpled silent heap.

STOP AND PREDICT

What will the machine do to Laurie and Andy?

The sick feeling was back, and one of my legs was trembling. I thought of my first sight of the Eiffel Tower, the summer my mother left and Ilse came to live with us—and my panicky feeling over the way it stretched so far up into the sky. This was as if the Eiffel Tower had moved—had smashed a house to bits and swallowed up a man . . . tossed a dog to its death the way you might throw away an apple core.

Time passed more draggingly than I ever remembered. I looked at my watch, and the

VOCABULARY

wriggled—twisted.
Eiffel Tower—very tall landmark in Paris, France.
draggingly—slowly.

RESPONSE NOTES

display read 05:56. I looked again after what seemed like half an hour, and it said 05:58. The sky was getting lighter and there was first a point of gold, then a sliver, finally a disk of sun rose beyond the ruins of the house. I looked at my watch again. It was 06:07.

Andy said, "Look!"

The legs hadn't moved but the capsule was tilting upwards, beginning a slow rotation. The row of panels was moving to the left. Soon we might be out of the field of vision and have a chance of sneaking away.

STOP AND PREDICT

What will the two of them do—run or stay there? Why?

But as the rotation continued, a second row of panels came into view. It could see all round.

When it had traversed a hundred and eighty degrees, the rotation stopped. After that, nothing happened. The monster just stayed there fixed, as leaden minutes crawled by.

VOCABULARY

sliver—narrow piece.
tilting—slanting.
rotation—circular motion.
traversed—moved.
leaden—long.

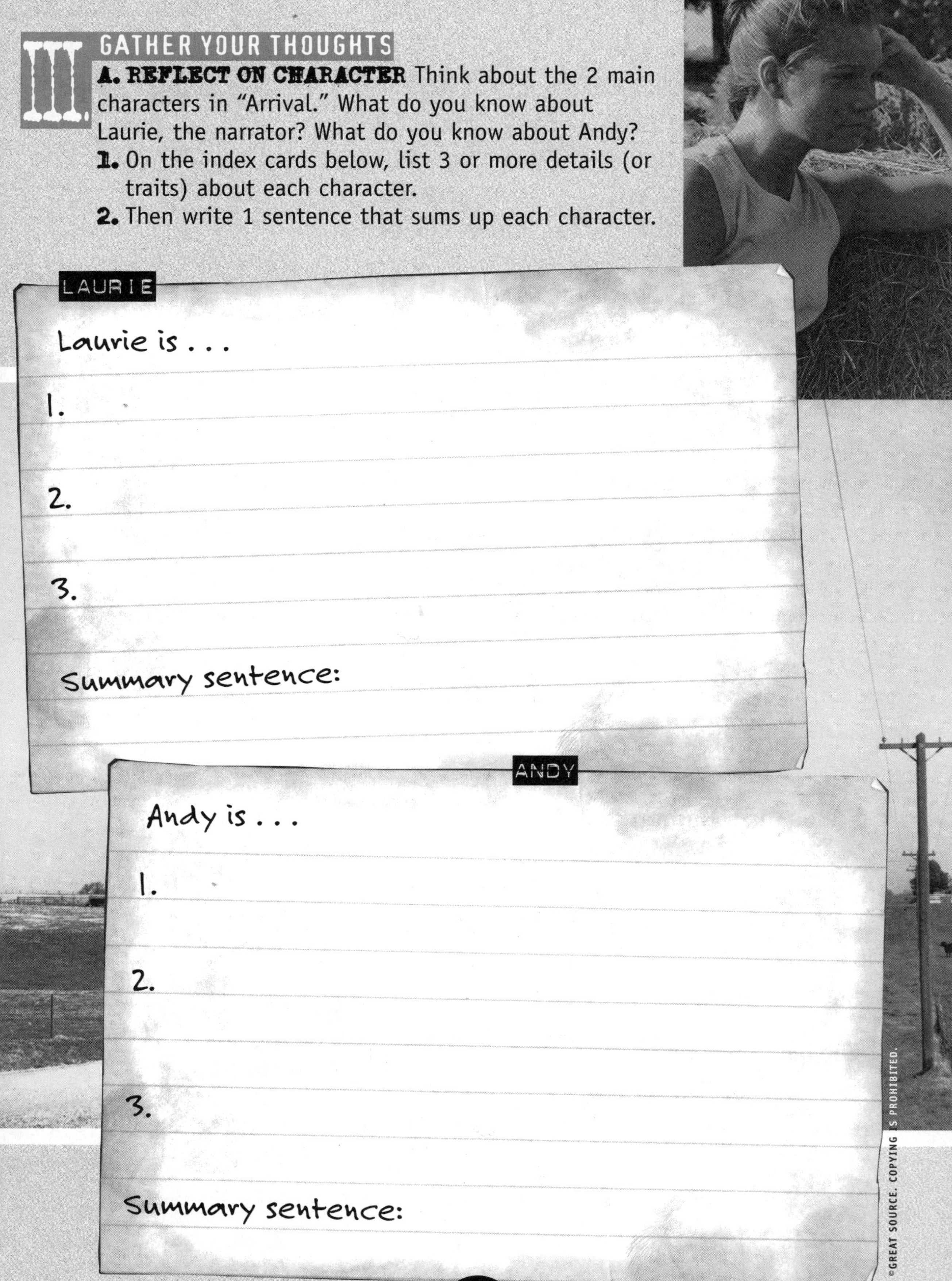

III. GATHER YOUR THOUGHTS

A. REFLECT ON CHARACTER Think about the 2 main characters in "Arrival." What do you know about Laurie, the narrator? What do you know about Andy?

1. On the index cards below, list 3 or more details (or traits) about each character.
2. Then write 1 sentence that sums up each character.

LAURIE

Laurie is . . .

1.

2.

3.

Summary sentence:

ANDY

Andy is . . .

1.

2.

3.

Summary sentence:

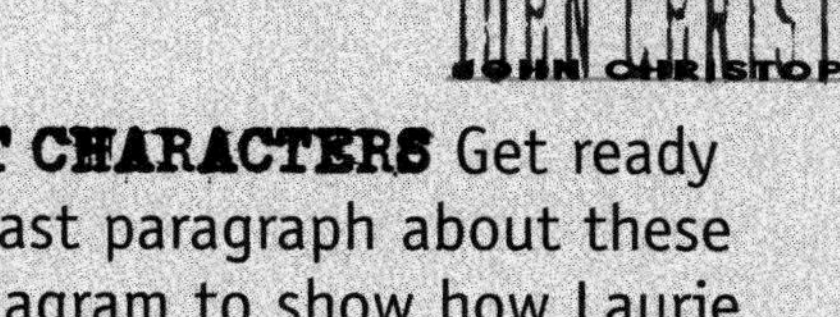

B. COMPARE AND CONTRAST CHARACTERS Get ready to write a compare and contrast paragraph about these 2 characters. Use the Venn diagram to show how Laurie and Andy are similar and how they're different.

1. Include such character traits as what they look like, how they feel, and how they act.
2. Use the middle part where the circles overlap to list traits the 2 characters have in common.

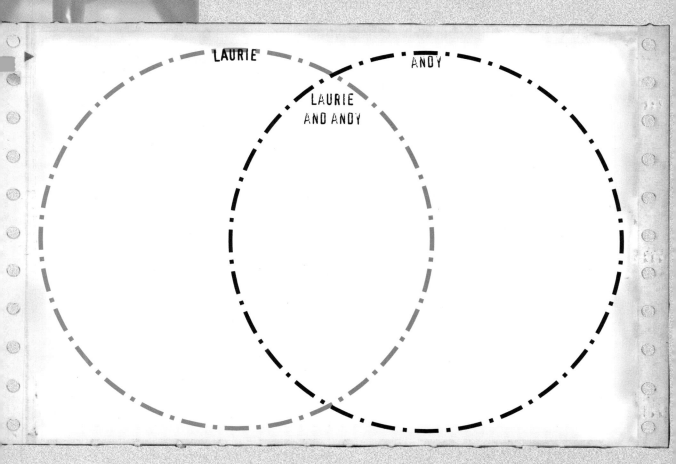

LAURIE

ANDY

LAURIE AND ANDY

C. WRITE A TOPIC SENTENCE Now write a topic sentence about Laurie and Andy. Your topic sentence should make it clear that you are going to compare and contrast the 2 characters.

my topic sentence:

IV. WRITE

Use your Venn diagram on the previous page to help you write a **compare and contrast paragraph.**

1. Start with your topic sentence.
2. Then give details about both characters. Remember to say what they have in common, as well as how they are different.
3. End with a closing sentence that sums up the comparison.
4. Use the Writers' Checklist to help you revise.

WRITERS' CHECKLIST

CONTRACTIONS

❑ **Did you use apostrophes correctly in your contractions? Remember that an apostrophe replaces the letter or letters that have been taken out.** EXAMPLES:
I + am = I'm
it + is = it's
they + are = they're
we + will = we'll

V. WRAP-UP

What did you like about John Christopher's style of writing? What didn't you like about it?

READERS' CHECKLIST

STYLE

- ❑ Did you find the passage well written?
- ❑ Are the sentences well constructed and the words well chosen?
- ❑ Does the style show you how to be a better writer?

Have you ever noticed that what is funny to one person isn't as funny to another? What makes something funny? Sometimes the answer has to do with point of view.

I. BEFORE YOU READ

With a partner, take a minute to recall what happened in the first part of "Arrival" on pages 105–113.

1. Then read each statement below in the Anticipation Guide.
2. Tell what you think about each statement. Listen to each other's point of view.
3. Finish by marking the number that shows how strongly you agree or disagree with the statement.

ANTICIPATION GUIDE

There is life on other planets.

1 2 3 4 5 6 7 8 9 10

strongly disagree — strongly agree

At some point in my life, I will encounter a being from another planet.

1 2 3 4 5 6 7 8 9 10

strongly disagree — strongly agree

I would like to visit another planet.

1 2 3 4 5 6 7 8 9 10

strongly disagree — strongly agree

I would like to find out more about galaxies beyond our own.

1 2 3 4 5 6 7 8 9 10

strongly disagree — strongly agree

Science-fiction stories always have some basis in fact.

1 2 3 4 5 6 7 8 9 10

strongly disagree — strongly agree

4. Now make a prediction: What do you think will happen to Laurie and Andy?

II. READ

Now read the second part of "Arrival."

1. As you read, jot down your **predictions** about character and plot in the Response Notes.
2. Pay special attention to the different viewpoints the characters have about what's happening.

"Arrival" (continued) from *When the Tripods Came* by John Christopher

RESPONSE NOTES

The first plane came over soon after eight. A fighter made two runs, east to west and then west to east at a lower level. The thing didn't move. A quarter of an hour later a helicopter circled round taking photographs, probably. It was nearly midday before the armored brigade arrived. Tanks and other tracked vehicles drew up on open farmland, and, in the bit of the farm lane in view, we could see an important-looking car and some trucks, including a TV van keeping a careful distance.

EXAMPLE: I don't think they will be able to talk with it.

After that, nothing happened for another long time. We learned later this was the period in which our side was attempting to make radio contact, trying different frequencies without result. Andy got impatient, and again suggested making a run for it, towards the tanks.

I said, "The fact it hasn't moved doesn't mean it won't. Remember the dog."

"I do. It might also decide to smash this hut."

"And if we run, and it starts something and the army starts something back . . . we're likely to catch it from both sides."

VOCABULARY

helicopter—aircraft with rotating blades.
armored brigade—armed military troops.
frequencies—signals.

RESPONSE NOTES

He reluctantly accepted that. "Why *hasn't* the army done something?"

"What do you think they ought to do?"

"Well, not just sit there."

"I suppose they don't want to rush things. . . ."

I broke off as an engine started up, followed by a rumble of tracks. We ran to the window. A single tank was moving forward. It had a pole attached to its turret, and a white flag fluttering from the pole.

The tank lurched across the field and stopped almost directly beneath the capsule. The engine switched off, and I heard a sparrow chirruping outside the shed. Then, unexpectedly, there was a burst of classical music.

I asked, "Where's that coming from?"

"From the tank, I think."

Fill in this Story Frame about what has happened so far. What 3 things did the army try to do?

STORY FRAME

1.

2.

3.

"But why?"

"Maybe they want to demonstrate that we're civilized, not barbarians. It's that bit from a Beethoven symphony, isn't it—the one that's sung as a European anthem?"

VOCABULARY

reluctantly—unwillingly; not wanting.
turret—towerlike structure for a gun.
lurched—rolled.
demonstrate—show.
civilized—cultured.
barbarians—wild; savage.
European anthem—song of praise for Europe.

"Arrival" CONTINUED

"That's crazy," I said.

"I don't know." Andy pointed. "Look."

The machine was showing signs of movement. Beneath the capsule a tentacle uncurled. It extended down towards the tank and began waving gently.

"What's it *doing*?" I asked.

"Maybe it's keeping time."

The weird thing was, he was right; it was moving in rhythm with the music. A second tentacle emerged, dipped, and brushed against the turret.

RESPONSE NOTES

How did the machine respond? Fill in 2 things it did.

STORY FRAME

4.

5.

As though it were getting the hang of things, the first tentacle started moving faster, in a more positive beat. The second felt its way round the tank from front to rear, then made a second approach from the side, moving over it and probing underneath. The tip dug down, rocking the tank slightly, and reemerged to complete an embrace. The tank rocked more violently as it was lifted, at first just clear of the ground, then sharply upward.

VOCABULARY

rhythm—time; pattern.
emerged—appeared.
probing—searching.
reemerged—reappeared.
embrace—enclosure.

RESPONSE NOTES

Abruptly the music gave way to the stridence of machine-gun fire. Tracer bullets flamed against the sky. The tank rose in the tentacle's grip until it was level with the panels. It hung there, spitting out sparks.

But pointlessly; at that angle the tracers were scouring empty sky. And they stopped abruptly, as the tentacle tightened its grip; armorplate crumpled like tinfoil. For two or three seconds it squeezed the tank, before uncurling and letting it drop. The tank fell like a stone, landing on its nose and balancing for an instant before toppling over. There was a furrow along the side where it had been compressed to less than half its original width.

Andy said, "That was a Challenger." He sounded shaken, but not as shaken as I felt. I could still see that terrible careless squeeze, the tank dropped like a toffee paper.

When I looked out again, one of the tentacles had retracted, but the other was waving still, and still in the rhythm it had picked up from the music. I wanted to run—somewhere, anywhere, not caring what came next—but I couldn't move a muscle. I wondered if anyone in the tank had survived. I didn't see how they could have.

Then, unexpectedly and shatteringly, there was a roar of aircraft as the fighter-bombers, which had been on standby, whooshed in from the south, launching rockets as they came. Of

VOCABULARY

stridence—harsh sound.
scouring—searching through.
tinfoil—thin sheet of aluminum used as wrapping.
toffee paper—candy wrapper.
whooshed—flew quickly.

the six they fired, two scored hits. I saw the long spindly legs shatter, the capsule tilt, and sway and crash. It landed between the ruins of the farmhouse and the wrecked tank, with an impact that shook the shed.

I could hardly believe how quickly it was over—and how completely. But there was the capsule lying on its side, with broken bits of leg sticking out. As we stared, a second wave of fighter-bombers swooped in, pulverizing the remains.

The school term started three weeks later. By then the big excitement—with Andy and me being interviewed on television and local radio and all that—was over, but people at school were still interested. They fired questions at us—mostly me, because Andy was less willing to talk. I talked too much and then regretted it. When Wild Bill brought the subject up in physics class, I no longer wanted to discuss it, least of all with him.

RESPONSE NOTES

What were the next 3 things that happened in the story? Write them below.

STORY FRAME

6.

7.

8.

VOCABULARY

pulverizing—destroying.

RESPONSE NOTES

He didn't look wild and his name wasn't Bill; he was a small, neat gray-haired man with a clipped voice and a sarcastic manner. His name was Hockey, and he had a habit of swinging round from the board and throwing whatever was in his hand—a piece of chalk usually—at someone he thought might be misbehaving behind his back. On one occasion it was the board eraser, which was wooden and quite heavy, and he hit a boy in the back row on the forehead. We called him Wild Bill Hockey after Wild Bill Hickock.

"Come on, Cordray," he said, "don't be shy. Now that you're famous you owe something to those of us who aren't." Some of the girls tittered. "The first person to see a Tripod, as I gather the media has decided we shall call them. . . . You'll be in the history books for that, even if not for the Nobel Prize in Physics."

There was more tittering. I'd been second from bottom the previous term.

"It throws an interesting light on national psychology," Wild Bill went on, "to consider the various reactions to man's first encounter with creatures from another part of the universe."

He had a tendency, which most of us encouraged, to launch into discourses on things that interested him, some of them quite remote from physics. I was happier still if it got him off my back.

VOCABULARY

sarcastic—bitter.
tittered—giggled.
tendency—habit.
discourses—discussions.
physics—the study of matter and energy.

"Arrival" CONTINUED

RESPONSE NOTES

He said, "As you know, there were three landings; one in the United States, in Montana, one in Kazakhstan in the Soviet Union, and Cordray's little show on the edge of Dartmoor. The landings were roughly simultaneous, ours in the middle of the night, the American late the previous evening and the Russian in time for breakfast.

"The Americans spotted theirs first, after tracking it in on radar, and just surrounded it and waited. The Russians located the one in their territory fairly quickly too, and promptly liquidated it with a rocket strike. We played Beethoven to ours, sent in a single tank, and then smashed it after it had destroyed the tank. Is that a testimony to British moderation? Cordray?"

1. Who are the main characters in "Arrival"?

2. Where does the action take place?

I said unwillingly, "I don't know, sir. After it wrecked the farmhouse, I didn't care how soon they finished it off."

VOCABULARY

simultaneous—done at the same time.
liquidated—melted; turned into liquid.
British moderation—unhurried and restrained way the British behave.

RESPONSE NOTES

"No, I don't suppose you did. But presumably you had no more notion than the military of what a pushover it was going to be. And that, of course, is the fascinating part." He ran his fingers through his thinning hair.

"When I was your age there was a war on. We had a physics class similar to this interrupted one afternoon by a V-2 rocket that landed a quarter of a mile away and killed fifteen people. It was alarming, but I didn't really find it *interesting*. What interested me more than the war was what I read in the science-fiction magazines of those days. Rockets being hurled from Germany to England to kill people struck me as dull, compared with the possibilities of their being used to take us across interplanetary space to discover exotic life forms—or maybe bring them here to us.

"Science-fiction writers have portrayed that second possibility in a variety of ways. We have read of, or more recently watched on screen, alien invaders of every shape and size, color and texture, from overgrown bloodsucking spiders to cuddly little creatures with long snouts. Their arrival has been shown as bringing both disaster and revelation. What no one anticipated was a Close Encounter of the Absurd Kind, a cosmic farce. Why do I say farce, Cordray?"

VOCABULARY

pushover—weakling.
interplanetary space—around the planets in space.
exotic life forms—unusual forms of life.
snouts—noses.
disaster and revelation—bad and good.
anticipated—expected.
cosmic farce—grand joke.

"Arrival" CONTINUED

"I don't know, sir."

"Well, you saw it, didn't you? Consider the Tripods themselves, for a start. What sort of goons would dream up something so clumsy and inefficient as a means of getting around?"

Hilda Goossens, a tall, bony redhead who was the class genius and his favorite, said, "But they must have had very advanced technology. We know they couldn't have come from within our solar system, so they must have traveled light-years to get here."

Wild Bill nodded. "Agreed. But consider further. Although the Americans didn't approach their Tripod, they did try the experiment of driving animals close in. Night had fallen by that time. And the Tripod switched on ordinary white light—searchlight beams, you could say—to find out what was happening beneath its feet. So it looks as though they don't even have infrared!

"And having gone to the considerable trouble of dropping these three machines at various

RESPONSE NOTES

VOCABULARY

goons—aliens.
inefficient—poorly managed.
light-years—trillions of years.
infrared—good visibility.

points of the planet, think of what they used them for. Two out of three just sat around; the third demolished a farmhouse and *then* sat around. And a single sortie from a single air force squadron was sufficient to reduce it to mechanical garbage. The other two put up no better defense; the one in America actually self-destructed without being attacked. In fact, altogether the dreaded invasion from outer space proved to be the comic show of the century."

1. What is the problem or conflict?

2. How is the conflict solved or resolved?

Some laughed. Although I'd done my bit of crawling to Wild Bill in the past, I didn't join in. I could still see it too clearly—the insectlike shape towering above the ruins of the farmhouse, the snaky tentacles plucking up pathetic bits and pieces and tossing them away. . . . It hadn't been funny then, and it wasn't now.

VOCABULARY

sortie—attack.

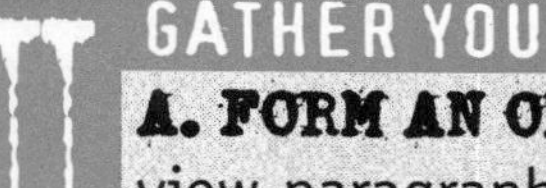

III. GATHER YOUR THOUGHTS

A. FORM AN OPINION Now prepare to write a point of view paragraph by forming an opinion of your own. Decide whether you agree or disagree with the following statement:

The chances of a spaceship from another planet landing in the United States are very slim.

AGREE DISAGREE

(circle one)

B. SUPPORT AN OPINION Use the organizer below to support your opinion. Write at least 3 or 4 statements that support your opinion.

1. My opinion:

2. Support for my opinion:

-
-
-
-

3. Concluding sentence:

IV. WRITE

Now write a **point of view paragraph**.

1. Begin with a sentence stating your opinion.
2. Then support your opinion using facts from your organizer and end with a sentence that sums up your point of view.
3. Use the Writers' Checklist as you revise.

WRITERS' CHECKLIST

COMMAS

- ❑ **Did you use commas to separate the items in a series of three or more?** EXAMPLE: *The tentacles were long, thin, and sharp.*
- ❑ **Did you use commas in dates between the month and the year or the day and the year?** EXAMPLE: *The spaceship landed November 16, 2002.*
- ❑ **Did you use commas in addresses to separate the city from state?** EXAMPLE: *The spaceship touched down in Cleveland, Ohio.*

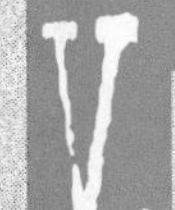

V. WRAP-UP

What things did John Christopher's story make you think about?

READERS' CHECKLIST

DEPTH

- ❑ **Did the story make you think about things?**
- ❑ **Did it set off thoughts beyond the surface topic?**

Facing Adversity

Most people are afraid of one thing or another. Life is full of frightening challenges that we must confront every day. When facing adversity, President Franklin Delano Roosevelt had the best advice. He said: "The only thing we have to fear is fear itself."

13: Life Doesn't Frighten Me

Good readers visualize. That is, they "see" things as they read. They make mental pictures of the persons, places, and things the writer describes. The pictures you create in your mind make it easier for you to "see" the author's ideas.

I. BEFORE YOU READ

Choose a reader who will read with expression.

1. Listen carefully as the reader reads the poem's title and first stanza. Try to visualize what's being described.
2. Then complete the Listener's Guide below.

"Life Doesn't Frighten Me"
by Maya Angelou

Shadows on the wall
Noises down the hall
Life doesn't frighten me at all
Bad dogs barking loud
Big ghosts in a cloud
Life doesn't frighten me at all.

MY LISTENER'S GUIDE

POEM TITLE:

Words or phrases that caught my attention:

This poem is about:

I predict the poem will be interesting / dull. (circle one)

I predict the poem will be easy / hard. (circle one)

READ

Now listen to the rest of "Life Doesn't Frighten Me."

1. **Visualize** the people, places, and things Angelou describes.
2. Draw sketches in the Response Notes.

"Life Doesn't Frighten Me" continued

Mean old Mother Goose
Lions on the loose
They don't frighten me at all
Dragons breathing flame
On my counterpane
That doesn't frighten me at all.

I go boo
Make them shoo
I make fun
Way they run
I won't cry
So they fly
I just smile
They go wild
Life doesn't frighten me at all.

Tough guys in a fight
All alone at night
Life doesn't frighten me at all.

RESPONSE NOTES

EXAMPLE:

STOP AND THINK

Why does the speaker name things like Mother Goose from nursery rhymes?

VOCABULARY

counterpane—bedspread.

RESPONSE NOTES

Panthers in the park
Strangers in the dark
No, they don't frighten me at all.

That new classroom where
Boys all pull my hair
(Kissy little girls
With their hair in curls)
They don't frighten me at all.

Don't show me frogs and snakes
And listen for my scream,
If I'm afraid at all
It's only in my dreams.

I've got a magic charm
That I keep up my sleeve,
I can walk the ocean floor
And never have to breathe.

Life doesn't frighten me at all
Not at all
Not at all.
Life doesn't frighten me at all.

STOP AND THINK

Why do you think the speaker names all the things she's not afraid of?

III. GATHER YOUR THOUGHTS

Organize Information Get ready to write an expository paragraph about Maya Angelou and "Life Doesn't Frighten Me." Your paragraph will be "published" in an encyclopedia of children's poetry.

1. First gather your facts.
2. Fill out the Fact Sheet about the poem.

FACT SHEET

Poem title: Poet's name:

What I know about this poet:

Is there rhyme?

examples:

Are there repeated words or phrases?

examples:

Are there words that appeal to the 5 senses?

examples:

Brief summary of what the poem is about:

The poet's main idea is:

IV. WRITE

Use your notes to help you write an **expository paragraph** about "Life Doesn't Frighten Me."

1. Explain who wrote the poem, how long it is, and what the language is like.
2. Then briefly summarize what the poem is about.
3. Use the Writers' Checklist to revise your writing.

WRITERS' CHECKLIST

CAPITALIZATION

- ❑ **Did you capitalize important words in the titles of books, poems, magazines, or articles?** EXAMPLE: *"Life Doesn't Frighten Me" was published after I Know Why the Caged Bird Sings.*
- ❑ **Did you use capital letters when naming a particular place?** EXAMPLE: *Let's go to Freehold Library.*

V. WRAP-UP

What is the poet's message or point in "Life Doesn't Frighten Me"?

READERS' CHECKLIST

UNDERSTANDING

- ❑ **Did you understand the reading?**
- ❑ **Was the message or point clear?**
- ❑ **Can you restate what the reading is about?**

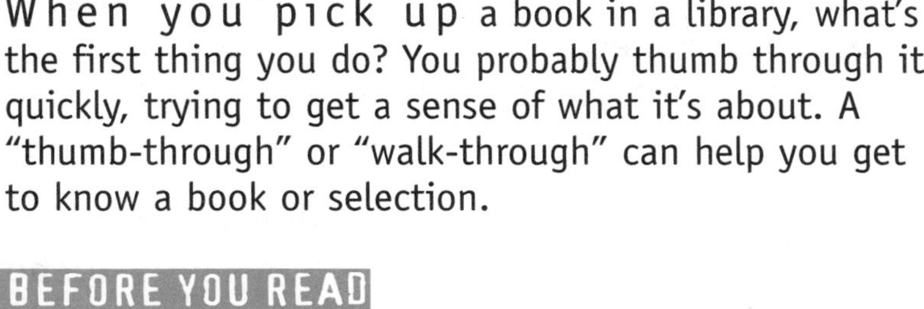

When you pick up a book in a library, what's the first thing you do? You probably thumb through it quickly, trying to get a sense of what it's about. A "thumb-through" or "walk-through" can help you get to know a book or selection.

I. BEFORE YOU READ

Read the title and first several paragraphs from the selection on the next page.

1. Then thumb through the rest of the selection.
2. Pay special attention to pictures, repeated words, character and place names, and the beginning and ending.
3. Make some notes on the chart below

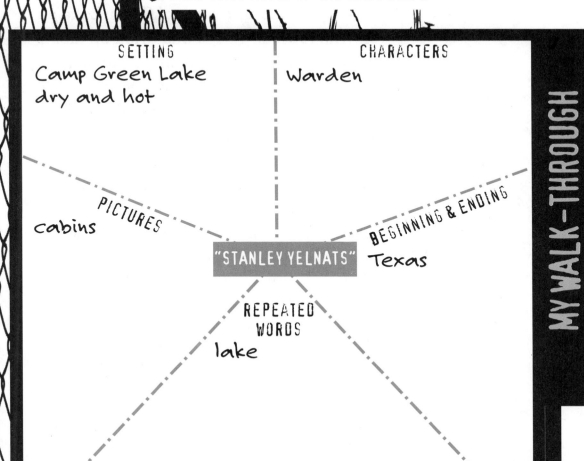

MY WALK-THROUGH

"STANLEY YELNATS"

SETTING
Camp Green Lake
dry and hot

CHARACTERS
Warden

PICTURES
cabins

BEGINNING & ENDING
Texas

REPEATED WORDS
lake

READ

Now read "Stanley Yelnats," the beginning of Louis Sachar's novel *Holes*.

1. Think about how Stanley's story makes you feel.
2. **React** to the selection. Jot down your feelings as you read. **Connect** what's being described to your own knowledge, feelings, and experiences.

RESPONSE NOTES

EXAMPLE:
Makes me think of pictures I've seen of dried-out land during heat waves.

"Stanley Yelnats" from *Holes*
by Louis Sachar

There is no lake at Camp Green Lake. There once was a very large lake here, the largest lake in Texas. That was over a hundred years ago. Now it is just a dry, flat wasteland.

There used to be a town of Green Lake as well. The town shriveled and dried up along with the lake, and the people who lived there.

During the summer the daytime temperature hovers around ninety-five degrees in the shade—if you can find any shade. There's not much shade in a big dry lake.

The only trees are two old oaks on the eastern edge of the "lake." A hammock is stretched between the two trees, and a log cabin stands behind that.

The campers are forbidden to lie in the hammock. It belongs to the Warden. The Warden owns the shade.

Out on the lake, rattlesnakes and scorpions find shade under rocks and in the holes dug by the campers.

VOCABULARY

shriveled—shrunk.
hovers—floats; remains.
hammock—hanging, easily swung cot.
scorpions—spider-like animals that have poisonous tails.

DOUBLE-ENTRY JOURNAL

Write your thoughts about the quote given. Then add a quotation from the story that you think is interesting and respond to it.

QUOTES	MY THOUGHTS
1. "The Warden owns the shade."	1.
2.	2.

"Stanley Yelnats" continued

RESPONSE NOTES

Here's a good rule to remember about rattlesnakes and scorpions: If you don't bother them, they won't bother you.

Usually.

Being bitten by a scorpion or even a rattlesnake is not the worst thing that can happen to you. You won't die.

Usually.

Sometimes a camper will try to be bitten by a scorpion, or even a small rattlesnake. Then he will get to spend a day or two recovering in his tent, instead of having to dig a hole out on the lake.

But you don't want to be bitten by a yellow-spotted lizard. That's the worst thing that can happen to you. You will die a slow and painful death.

Always.

If you get bitten by a yellow-spotted lizard, you might as well go into the shade of the oak trees and lie in the hammock.

RESPONSE NOTES

There is nothing anyone can do to you anymore.

The reader is probably asking: Why would anyone go to Camp Green Lake?

Most campers weren't given a choice. Camp Green Lake is a camp for bad boys.

If you take a bad boy and make him dig a hole every day in the hot sun, it will turn him into a good boy.

That was what some people thought.

Stanley Yelnats was given a choice. The judge said, "You may go to jail, or you may go to Camp Green Lake."

DOUBLE-ENTRY JOURNAL

Select and then respond to 2 more quotations from the story.

QUOTES	MY THOUGHTS
1.	1.
2.	2.

Stanley was from a poor family. He had never been to camp before.

Stanley Yelnats was the only passenger on the bus, not counting the driver or the guard.

The guard sat next to the driver with his seat turned around facing Stanley. A rifle lay across his lap.

RESPONSE NOTES

Stanley was sitting about ten rows back, handcuffed to his armrest. His backpack lay on the seat next to him. It contained his toothbrush, toothpaste, and a box of stationery his mother had given him. He'd promised to write to her at least once a week.

He looked out the window, although there wasn't much to see—mostly fields of hay and cotton. He was on a long bus ride to nowhere. The bus wasn't air-conditioned, and the hot, heavy air was almost as stifling as the handcuffs.

Stanley and his parents had tried to pretend that he was just going away to camp for a while, just like rich kids do. When Stanley was younger he used to play with stuffed animals, and pretend the animals were at camp. Camp Fun and Games he called it. Sometimes he'd have them play soccer with a marble. Other times they'd run an obstacle course, or go bungee jumping off a table, tied to broken rubber bands. Now Stanley tried to pretend he was going to Camp Fun and Games. Maybe he'd make some friends, he thought. At least he'd get to swim in the lake.

He didn't have any friends at home. He was overweight and the kids at his middle school often teased him about his size. Even his teachers sometimes made cruel comments

VOCABULARY

stationery—materials used in writing.
stifling—suffocating.

RESPONSE NOTES

without realizing it. On his last day of school, his math teacher, Mrs. Bell, taught ratios. As an example, she chose the heaviest kid in the class and the lightest kid in the class, and had them weigh themselves. Stanley weighed three times as much as the other boy. Mrs. Bell wrote the ratio on the board, 3:1, unaware of how much embarrassment she had caused both of them.

Stanley was arrested later that day.

DOUBLE-ENTRY JOURNAL

Write your thoughts and feelings about these 3 topics in the right-hand column.

TOPICS	MY THOUGHTS
Stanley Yelnats	
Camp Green Lake	
the Warden	

VOCABULARY

ratios—equations comparing relative sizes of two objects.

III. GATHER YOUR THOUGHTS

Holes is a young boy's account of what happened when he was sent to reform school for a crime he didn't commit.

A. CONNECT Think of a time you were punished for something you didn't do. What happened? Write 1-2 sentences describing the event.

B. GATHER DETAILS Now list 3 details that will help you write a journal entry about what happened.

EXAMPLE:

SUBJECT FOR JOURNAL ENTRY the day my friend broke my dad's camera

DETAIL #1 playing around in the garage

DETAIL #2 sweeping up and hiding the pieces

DETAIL #3 getting grounded

SUBJECT FOR JOURNAL ENTRY

DETAIL #1

DETAIL #2

DETAIL #3

IV. WRITE

Now write a **journal entry**.

1. Remember to use plenty of detail.
2. Write in the first-person (*I* said, *we* thought).
3. Use the Writers' Checklist to help you revise.

date

Dear Journal,

WRITERS' CHECKLIST

EASILY CONFUSED WORDS

- ❑ **Did you correctly use the words *it's* and *its*? *It's* is a contraction for *it is*. *Its* is the possessive form of *it*.** EXAMPLES: ***It's the funniest book I've read. Its cover makes me laugh.***
- ❑ **Did you correctly use the words *their*, *there*, and *they're*? *Their* is a possessive pronoun used to indicate ownership. Use *there* to point out a location and *they're* as the contraction for *they are*.** EXAMPLES: ***Holes is their book. They're upset because we left the book there.***

V. WRAP-UP

What did "Stanley Yelnats" mean to you?

READERS' CHECKLIST

MEANING

- ❑ **Did you learn something from the reading?**
- ❑ **Did it affect you or make an impression?**

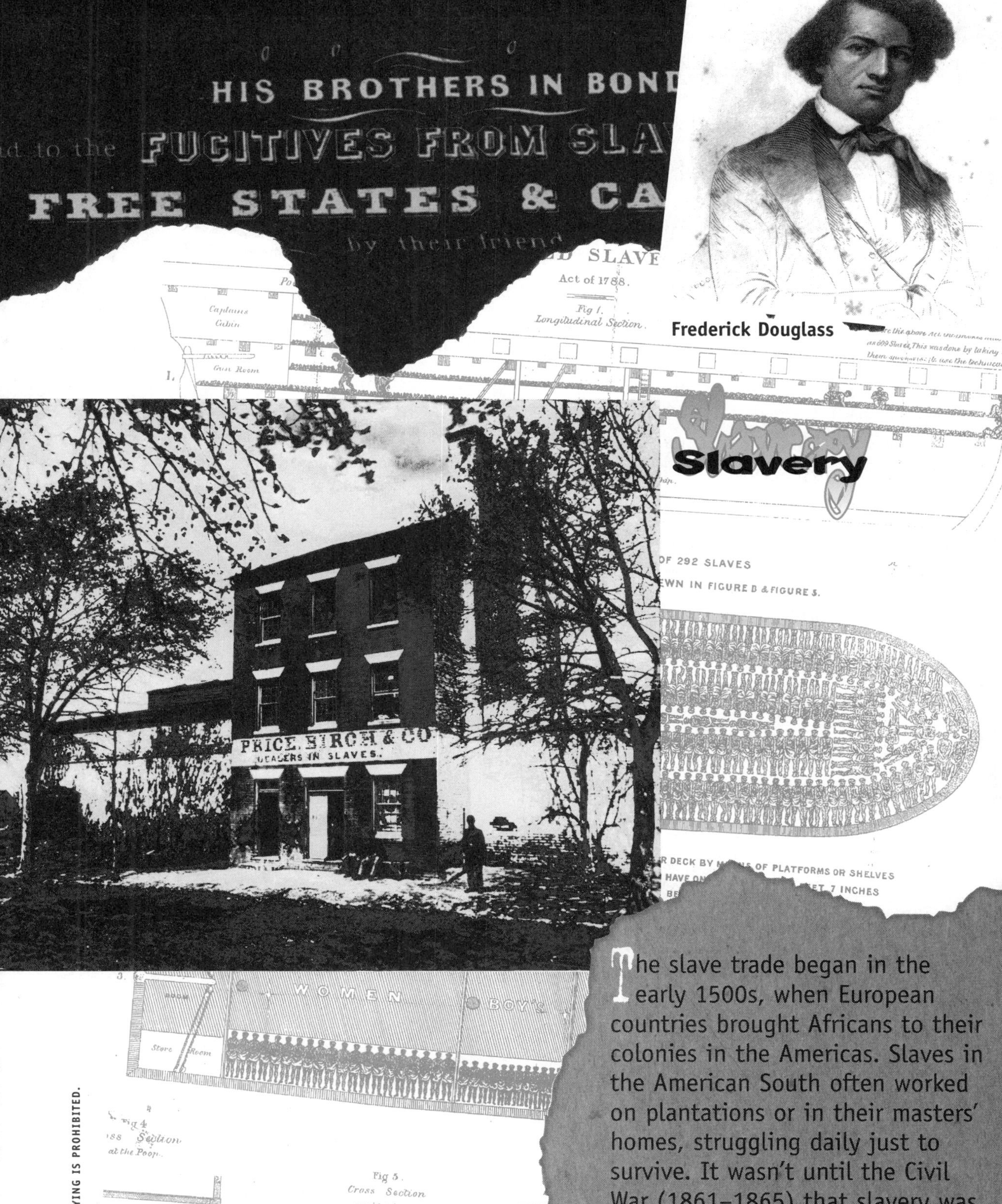

Frederick Douglass

Slavery

The slave trade began in the early 1500s, when European countries brought Africans to their colonies in the Americas. Slaves in the American South often worked on plantations or in their masters' homes, struggling daily just to survive. It wasn't until the Civil War (1861–1865) that slavery was finally ended. The struggle to maintain that freedom, however, would go on for many years.

15: The Revolt of Denmark Vesey

What do events in the past mean to us today? How do these events relate to you and your life? Denmark Vesey was an African-American slave who was able to buy his freedom in 1799. How does what happened to him relate to you today?

I. BEFORE YOU READ

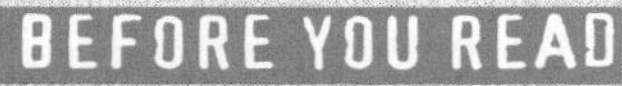

Take a picture walk through the selection. It can familiarize you with what you are about to read.

1. Look at the pictures carefully.
2. Jot down your questions and reactions.
3. Make a prediction about the selection's content.

PICTURE WALK

THESE PICTURES REMIND ME OF:

I HAVE THESE QUESTIONS ABOUT THE PICTURES:

TO ME, THE MOST MEMORABLE PICTURE IS:

I PREDICT THE SELECTION WILL BE ABOUT:

REGULATED SLAVE TRADE

Act of 1788.

Fig I.
Longitudinal Section.

II. READ

Now read "The Revolt of Denmark Vesey."

1. As you read, think of **questions** you have about what's happening.
2. Write your questions in the Response Notes.

"The Revolt of Denmark Vesey" by Lila Perl

Denmark Vesey could hardly believe his good luck. Again and again he carefully read the numbers on the lottery ticket he held in his hand. It was true! They were the same as the winning numbers posted in the East Bay Street lottery office in Charleston, South Carolina. All Denmark Vesey had to do was to go up to the window, present his ticket, and collect his money—the unimaginably large sum of fifteen hundred dollars.

This was a great deal of money for just about any ordinary person in South Carolina in the year 1799. But it was especially unusual for a black slave to come into such wealth. For one thing, very few slaves had any money of their own, much less enough to buy a lottery ticket. Also, most of the hundred thousand slaves who lived in South Carolina in the late 1700s labored on the rice, indigo, and cotton plantations, located some distance inland from the bustling port city of Charleston, where lottery tickets could be bought.

Denmark Vesey, however, was not a plantation slave. For eighteen years he'd

RESPONSE NOTES

EXAMPLE: How did he learn to read? Did he go to school?

VOCABULARY

lottery ticket—sheet of paper used in a contest to win money.
unimaginably—unbelievably.
indigo—shrub that produces a blue dye.
bustling port city—busy and active city where ships load and unload.

BE SOLD on boa
ip *Bance-Island*, on tuesda
next, at *Ashley-Ferry*;
rgo of about 250 fine h
NEGROES
just arrived from the
Windward & Rice Coast
—The utmost care has

RESPONSE NOTES

belonged to a sea captain named Joseph Vesey. Captain Vesey was a slave trader who'd grown wealthy importing slaves from Africa to the Caribbean and the American South. In 1781, on one of his trips from the Danish colony of Saint Thomas to another Caribbean island, he'd picked up a fourteen-year-old youth whom he named Denmark. The boy became a personal servant to Captain Vesey and, as was the custom, he was given his master's second name.

STOP AND THINK

What have you learned so far about Denmark Vesey?

Between 1781 and 1783, Denmark Vesey sailed with the captain. He'd watched the bewildered and shackled blacks of West Africa driven aboard the slave ship and packed into tightly cramped quarters like so much cargo. He'd witnessed the filth, disease, and inhuman treatment that caused as many as one-third of the captives to die and be tossed overboard before the voyage was completed. And he'd seen the despair and humiliation of those who survived to reach port as they stood on the

OF LOWER DECK WITH THE STOWAGE OF 292 SLAVES
STOWED UNDER THE SHELVES AS SHEWN IN FIGURE B & FIG
NAL SLAVES ROUND THE WINGS OR SIDES OF THE LOWER DECK BY MEANS OF
THE SLAVES STOWED ON THE SHELVES AND BELOW THEM HAVE ONLY A HEIGHT
BETWEEN THE BEAMS: AND FAR LESS UNDER THE BEAMS. See Fig 1.

VOCABULARY

bewildered—confused.
shackled—chained.
cargo—freight carried by a ship.
captives—people held against their will.
humiliation—feelings of shame.

RESPONSE NOTES

auction block, waiting to be sold to the highest bidder.

Then, as the American Revolution ended in 1783, things changed for the better for Denmark Vesey. The captain decided to retire from the slave trade. He moved to Charleston and went into the business of furnishing supplies for ships being readied to sail to ports all over the world. Denmark Vesey, as one of eight slave servants in the Captain's household, became a skilled carpenter. The captain even hired him out to other Charleston residents and gave him a little money in addition to his keep. This money enabled Denmark Vesey to try his luck in the lottery, and now the money he had won would take him a step further. With six hundred dollars he could buy his freedom from Captain Vesey and join the thousand or so free blacks who lived in the city of Charleston.

STOP AND THINK

How does Vesey plan to buy his freedom?

In January of 1800, a month after the lottery, the captain gave Denmark Vesey his papers of emancipation. With the remainder of his winnings he was able to buy himself a small house in Charleston. And along with other free blacks, who worked as cooks, nurses,

VOCABULARY

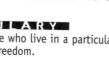

residents—people who live in a particular place permanently.
emancipation—freedom.

RESPONSE NOTES

seamstresses, bricklayers, fishermen, and blacksmiths, he was able to earn a living hiring himself out freely as a carpenter.

Life was much improved for Denmark Vesey. It was not perfect, of course, for free blacks did not share equal status with whites. They had to be very careful to carry their papers with them at all times lest they be resold into slavery. They had to pay special taxes for the privilege of living in Charleston, and if accused of a crime, they could not testify against a white person. So they banded together to protect themselves in special fellowship and church groups.

They also read and discussed the writings of the antislavery leaders of the day. Not all abolitionists lived in the northern states. In Charleston itself there were whites who opposed slavery. Among the most outspoken were the Grimké sisters, Sarah and Angelina. And on the French-owned Caribbean island of St. Domingue, there had actually been a successful slave revolt in 1804. The now independent island republic was known as Haiti.

As Denmark Vesey thought of this event, he could not wipe from his memory the scenes he'd beheld on the slave ship of his former master. Infuriating too was the fact that in 1807 the importation of slaves into the United States had been declared illegal. Yet the law was not

VOCABULARY

seamstresses—people who make their livings sewing.
status—social position.
abolitionists—people who opposed slavery.
Infuriating—angering.
importation—bringing in from abroad for the sale.

RESPONSE NOTES

enforced, because the plantation owners who were profiting from the boom in cotton demanded more and more black slave labor.

By 1821 Denmark Vesey felt himself driven to take action. Carefully he began to enlist the help of cool, courageous, and well-organized blacks, some slave and some free. The network began to recruit support from within Charleston, at that time the sixth-largest city in the United States, and well beyond it. For Denmark Vesey planned nothing short of a rebellion that would free slaves not only in South Carolina but throughout the United States.

STOP AND THINK

What leads Vesey to plan a revolt?

He saw himself as favored by fortune in having become free, educated, and prosperous. Now, at the age of fifty-four, he must try to lift the burden that other Africans endured under slavery.

Vesey and other free blacks contributed money to buy weapons and horses, which were hidden away in readiness for the uprising. By the time a date—July 14, 1822—had been set for the revolt, there were said to be nine thousand

VOCABULARY

boom—growth; increase.
prosperous—successful.

followers secretly sworn to the movement.

But the revolt in Denmark Vesey's heart and mind was never to become a reality. Sometime in May 1822 word leaked out through a house slave who had been frightened and told his master. Vesey decided to move the date up from July 14 to June 16, in case there were any more leaks. But it was already too late. The Charleston authorities had been put on the alert.

Although the authorities were never able to identify most of the members of the movement, its leaders were caught and tried. On July 2, 1822, Denmark Vesey paid with his life for the freedom he had hoped to share with others. True, his plans had called for fighting violence with violence. But as the Civil War was to prove some forty years later, there was to be no peaceful way of ending human enslavement.

VOCABULARY

authorities—people in charge, like police officers and other such city leaders.
enslavement—slavery.

STOP AND THINK

What happens to Vesey's revolt?

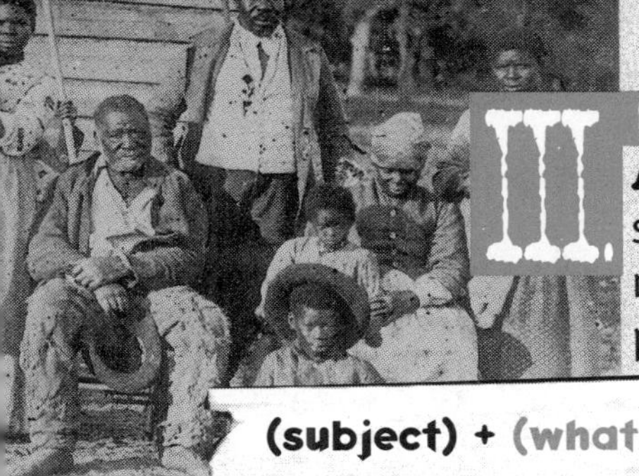

III. GATHER YOUR THOUGHTS

A. FIND THE MAIN IDEA Get ready to write a summary of the selection you just read. First you'll need to find the main idea. To find the main idea of a piece of writing, use this formula.

(subject) + (what the author says about the subject) = main idea.

1. Write the subject in the middle of the web.
2. On the arms, write some things the author says about the subject.
3. Circle the idea that seems the most important.

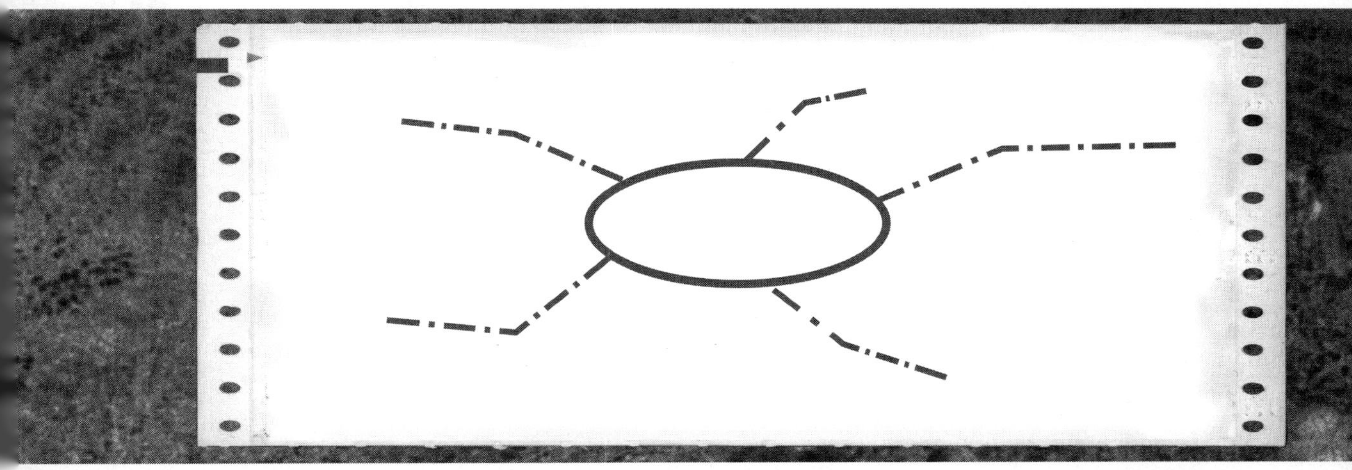

B. LIST DETAILS List 3 or 4 important details Perl uses to support the main idea you selected above.

EXAMPLE:

1.

2.

3.

4.

IV. WRITE

Write a **summary** of "The Revolt of Denmark Vesey."

1. Refer to the main idea and supporting details you listed on the previous page.
2. Use the Writers' Checklist to help you revise.

WRITERS' CHECKLIST

COMMAS

- ❑ **Did you use a comma between coordinate adjectives not joined by *and*?**
  EXAMPLES: **The angry, frightened crowd moved quickly. The angry and frightened crowd moved quickly.**

WRAP-UP

In your opinion, was "The Revolt of Denmark Vesey" easy or difficult to read? Why?

READERS' CHECKLIST

EASE

- ❑ **Was the passage easy to read?**
- ❑ **Were you able to read it smoothly and without difficulty?**

16: Born into Slavery

Have you ever wondered what it would be like to have lived long ago? What if you lived during the time of slavery and the Civil War? Reading gives you the chance to hear from people who lived long ago.

I. BEFORE YOU READ

With a partner, take turns reading these sentences aloud from "Born into Slavery."

1. Decide which sentence comes first, which comes next, and so on. Number them.
2. Then discuss with your partner how the sentences make you feel. Answer the questions below.

THINK-PAIR-SHARE

____ "I do not recollect of ever seeing my mother by the light of day."

____ "Frequently, before the child has reached its twelfth month, its mother is taken from it, and hired out on some farm a considerable distance off. . . ."

____ "My mother and I were separated when I was but an infant—before I knew her as my mother."

____ "The opinion was also whispered that my master was my father; but of the correctness of this opinion, I know nothing. . . ."

____ "I do not remember to have ever met a slave who could tell of his birthday."

These sentences make me feel:

____

____

They make my reading partner feel:

____

____

II. READ

Now read Frederick Douglass's account of his childhood.

1. **Mark** or **highlight** parts that help you understand what it was like to be a slave.
2. Note your ideas and comments in the Response Notes.

"Born into Slavery" from *Narrative of the Life of Frederick Douglass, an American Slave* by Frederick Douglass

RESPONSE NOTES

I was born in Tuckahoe, near Hillsborough, and about twelve miles from Easton, in Talbot county, Maryland. I have no accurate knowledge of my age, never having seen any authentic record containing it. By far the larger part of the slaves know as little of their ages as horses know of theirs, and it is the wish of most masters within my knowledge to keep their slaves thus ignorant. I do not remember to have ever met a slave who could tell of his birthday. They seldom come nearer to it than planting-time, harvest-time, cherry-time, spring-time, or fall-time. A want of information concerning my own was a source of unhappiness to me even during childhood. The white children could tell their ages. I could not tell why I ought to be deprived of the same privilege. I was not allowed to make any inquiries of my master concerning it.

EXAMPLE: Must be horrible not to know your age.

VOCABULARY

authentic record—document; written proof.
want—desire; need.
deprived—prevented from having.
inquiries—questions.

stop and think

Why do you think slave masters refused to give a slave's age?

RESPONSE NOTES

"Born into Slavery" CONTINUED

He deemed all such inquiries on the part of a slave improper and impertinent, and evidence of a restless spirit. The nearest estimate I can give makes me now between twenty-seven and twenty-eight years of age. I come to this from hearing my master say, some time during 1835, I was about seventeen years old.

My mother was named Harriet Bailey. She was the daughter of Isaac and Betsey Bailey, both colored, and quite dark. My mother was of a darker complexion than either my grandmother or grandfather.

My father was a white man. He was admitted to be such by all I ever heard speak of my parentage. The opinion was also whispered that my master was my father; but of the correctness of this opinion, I know nothing; the means of knowing was withheld from me. My mother and I were separated when I was but an infant—before I knew her as my mother. It is a common custom, in the part of Maryland from which I ran away, to part children from their mothers at a very early age. Frequently, before the child has

VOCABULARY

impertinent—disrespectful.
complexion—skin color.
custom—thing that people usually do.

RESPONSE NOTES

reached its twelfth month, its mother is taken from it, and hired out on some farm a considerable distance off, and the child is placed under the care of an old woman, too old for hard labor. For what this separation is done, I do not know, unless it be to hinder the development of the child's affection toward its mother, and to blunt and destroy the natural affection of the mother for the child. This is the inevitable result.

stop and think

From what you've read, how does Douglass feel about his mother?

....

....

....

I never saw my mother, to know her as such, more than four or five times in my life; and each of these times was very short in duration, and at night. She was hired by a Mr. Stewart, who lived about twelve miles from my home. She made her journeys to see me in the night, travelling the whole distance on foot, after the performance of her day's work. She was a field hand, and a whipping is the penalty of not being in the field at sunrise, unless a slave has special

VOCABULARY

hinder—block; obstruct.
affection—feeling of love.
blunt—make less strong.
inevitable—unavoidable.
duration—length of time.

RESPONSE NOTES

permission from his or her master to the contrary—a permission which they seldom get, and one that gives to him the proud name of being a kind master. I do not recollect of ever seeing my mother by the light of day. She was with me in the night. She would lie down with me, and get me to sleep, but long before I waked she was gone. Very little communication ever took place between us. Death soon ended what little we could have while she lived, and with it her hardships and suffering. She died when I was about seven years old, on one of my master's farms, near Lee's Mill. I was not allowed to be present during her illness, at her death, or burial. She was gone long before I knew any thing about it. Never having enjoyed, to any considerable extent, her soothing presence, her tender and watchful care, I received the tidings of her death with much the same emotions I should have probably felt at the death of a stranger.

VOCABULARY

recollect—remember.
tidings—news.

stop and think

How does Douglass feel when he hears his mother has died?

GATHER YOUR THOUGHTS

A. REFLECT After reading, stop for a moment to reflect on what Douglass described.

1. Why were slave children separated from their mothers?

2. What effect did the separation have?

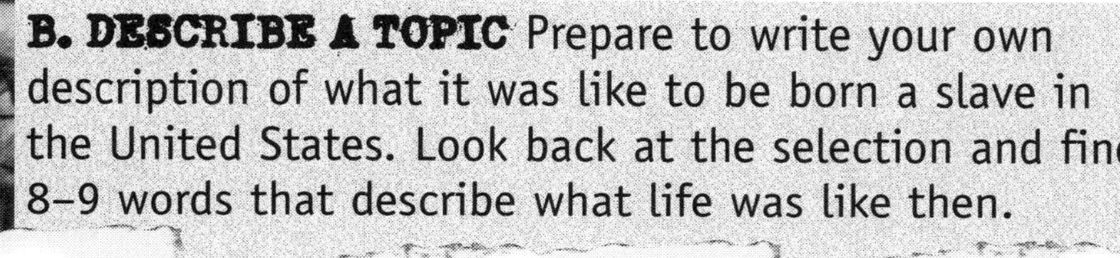

B. DESCRIBE A TOPIC Prepare to write your own description of what it was like to be born a slave in the United States. Look back at the selection and find 8–9 words that describe what life was like then.

C. PLAN Start planning your descriptive paragraph.

1. Draft a topic sentence.
2. It should state your overall point about what it was like to be born a slave.

IV. WRITE

Now write a **descriptive paragraph** of what it was like to be born a slave in the United States.

1. Start with a topic sentence and give specific details.
2. Use the Writers' Checklist to help you revise.

WRITERS' CHECKLIST

USAGE

- ❑ **Did you use *good* as an adjective and *well* as an adverb?** EXAMPLES: *That is a good idea.* (*Good* modifies the noun *idea.*) *José works well.* (*Well* modifies the verb *works*)
- ❑ **Did you use *better* to mean "more desirable" and *best* to mean "most desirable"?** EXAMPLE: *Her project is better than mine, but his is the best one in the class.*

V. WRAP-UP

What did you find most interesting about "Born into Slavery"?

READERS' CHECKLIST

ENJOYMENT

- ❑ **Did you like the reading?**
- ❑ **Was the reading experience pleasurable?**
- ❑ **Would you want to reread the piece?**

Victor Martinez

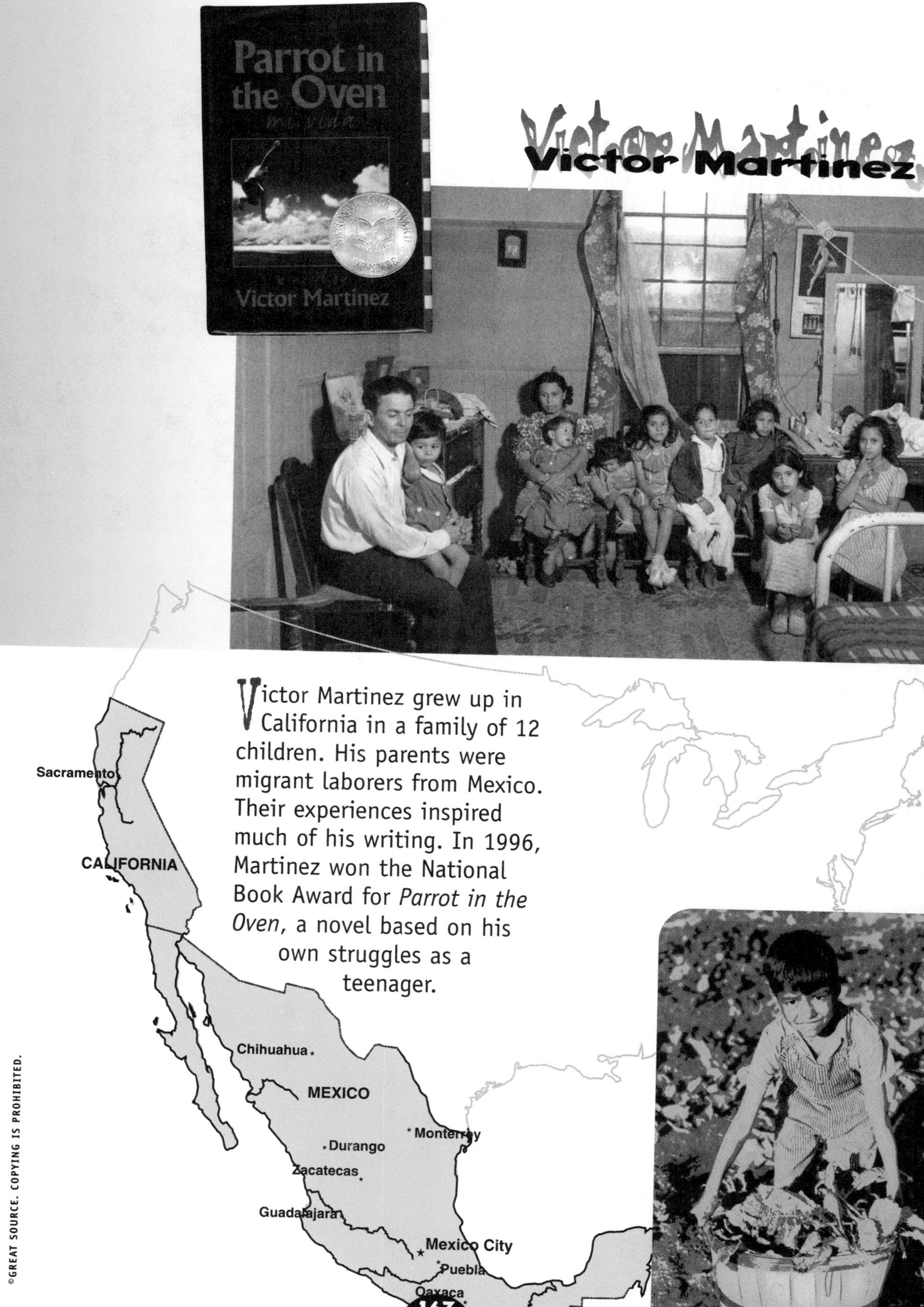

Victor Martinez grew up in California in a family of 12 children. His parents were migrant laborers from Mexico. Their experiences inspired much of his writing. In 1996, Martinez won the National Book Award for *Parrot in the Oven*, a novel based on his own struggles as a teenager.

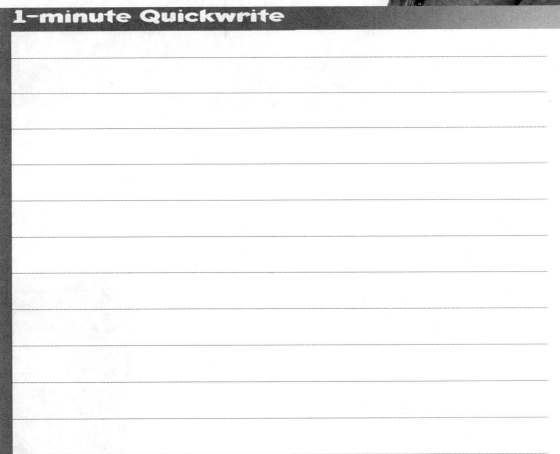

Do you know anyone who drives you just a little bit crazy? Is he or she a "character"? Literature is filled with strange and unusual characters. Reading about them makes us think about why people act the way they do.

I. BEFORE YOU READ

Think of why you act the way you do.

1. Then do a quickwrite for 1 minute. Tell about something you did recently and why you did it.
2. Write everything you can think of.

1-minute Quickwrite

II. READ

Now read "Nardo," an excerpt from Victor Martinez's novel *Parrot in the Oven*.

1. As you read, **clarify** why the main character acts the way he does.
2. Write your thoughts in the Response Notes.

Response Notes

"Nardo" from *Parrot in the Oven* by Victor Martinez

That summer my brother, Bernardo, or "Nardo," as we call him, flipped through more jobs than a thumb through a deck of cards. First he was a dishwasher, then a busboy, then a parking attendant and, finally, a patty turner for some guy who never seemed to be in his hamburger stand for more than ten minutes at a time. (Mom believed he sold marijuana, or did some other illegal shamelessness.) Nardo lost one job for not showing up regular enough, another for showing up too regular—the boss hated his guts. The last job lost him when the owner of the hamburger stand packed up unexpectedly and left for Canada.

EXAMPLE: Nardo must not care about pleasing the boss.

The job Nardo misses most, though, was when he worked as a busboy for the Bonneville Lakes Golf and Catering Service. He says it was the only time he ever got to touch elbows with rich people. The parties they catered served free daiquiris, whisky drinks, and cold beer, really cold, in big barrels choking with

VOCABULARY

busboy—person who clears tables in a restaurant.
patty turner—person who flips burgers at a restaurant.
marijuana—an illegal drug.
daiquiris—fruity alcoholic drinks.

Response Notes

ice. At some parties, like the one he got fired from, they passed out tickets for juicy prizes like motorcycles, TV sets, stereos and snow skis. The last party had a six-piece band and a great huge dance floor so the "old fogies," as my brother called them, could get sloshed and make fools of themselves.

As it turns out, he and a white guy named Randy took off their busboy jackets and began daring each other to get a ticket and ask a girl to dance.

stop+predict

What will happen if Nardo goes through with the dare?

stop+predict

Randy bet Nardo wouldn't do it, and Nardo bet he would, and after a two-dollar pledge he steered for the ticket lady.

"I could've hashed it around a bit, you know, Manny," he said. "I could've double- and triple-dared the guy a couple of times over, then come up with a good excuse. But that ain't my style."

Instead he tapped Randy's fingers smooth as fur and walked up to the ticket lady. She peered out from behind the large butcher-paper-covered table at the blotches of pasta

VOCABULARY

stereos—machine that plays musical records and tapes.
fogies—out-of-date, old-fashioned people.
sloshed—drunk.
blotches—stains; spots.

Response Notes

sauce on his black uniform pants and white shirt—which were supposed to go clean with the catering service's light orange busboy jacket, but didn't—and said, "Ah, what the hell," and tore him out a tag.

Before the little voice nagging inside him could talk louder, Nardo asked the nearest girl for a dance. She had about a million freckles and enough wire in her mouth to run a toy train over. They stumbled around the dance floor until the band mercifully ground to a halt. She looked down at his arm kind of shylike and said, "You dance real nice."

stop+predict

What will Nardo do now?

....

....

....

Now my brother had what you could call a sixth sense. "*Es muy vivo*," as my grandma used to say about a kid born that way, and with Nardo it was pretty much a scary truth. He could duck trouble better than a champion boxer could duck a right cross. He made hairline escapes from baths, belt whippings, and scoldings just by not being around when punishment came through the door. So I

VOCABULARY

catering service's—belonging to the food serving business.
ground to a halt—stopped.
Es muy vivo—Spanish for "He's very alert."
right cross—name for a boxer's punch thrown with the right hand.

believed him when he said something ticklish crawled over his shoulder, and when he turned around, there, across the dance floor, in front of the bandleader about to make an announcement over the microphone, was his boss, Mr. Baxter—and boy was he steamed!

Mr. Baxter owned the catering service, and sometimes, my brother said, the way he'd yell at the busboys, it was like he owned them, too.

stop+predict

What do you think Mr. Baxter will say to Nardo?

stop+predict

Mr. Baxter didn't say anything, just pointed to the door, then at Nardo, and scratched a big X across his chest. Just like that, he was fired.

The way Nardo tells it, you'd think he did that man a favor working for him. "Don't you ever get braces, Manny," he said, as if that were the lesson he'd learned.

VOCABULARY
steamed—angry.

stop+predict

What will happen to Nardo next?

III. GATHER YOUR THOUGHTS

A. REFLECT ON CHARACTER Identify 3-4 things that describe the character of Nardo.

1. Put 1 word to describe him on the line in each circle.

2. Then list an example from the story that supports each descriptive word.

daring

challenges other busboy to ask a girl to dance

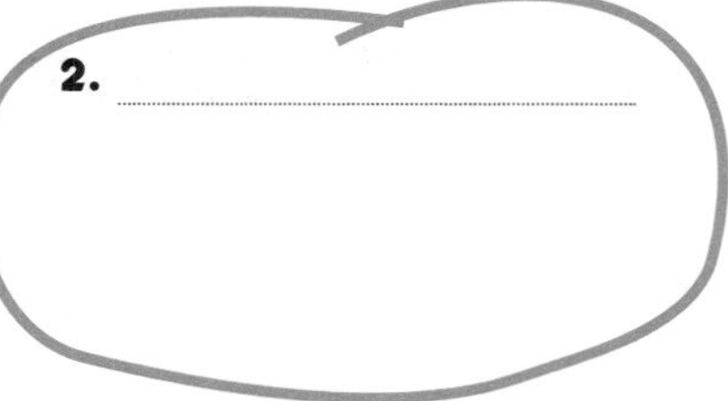

2. ______

3. ______

Nardo

4. ______

5. ______

B. CONNECT Now name 5 descriptive words that apply to you.

1. Write 1 word in each circle.

2. List an event or incident from your own life that supports your description.

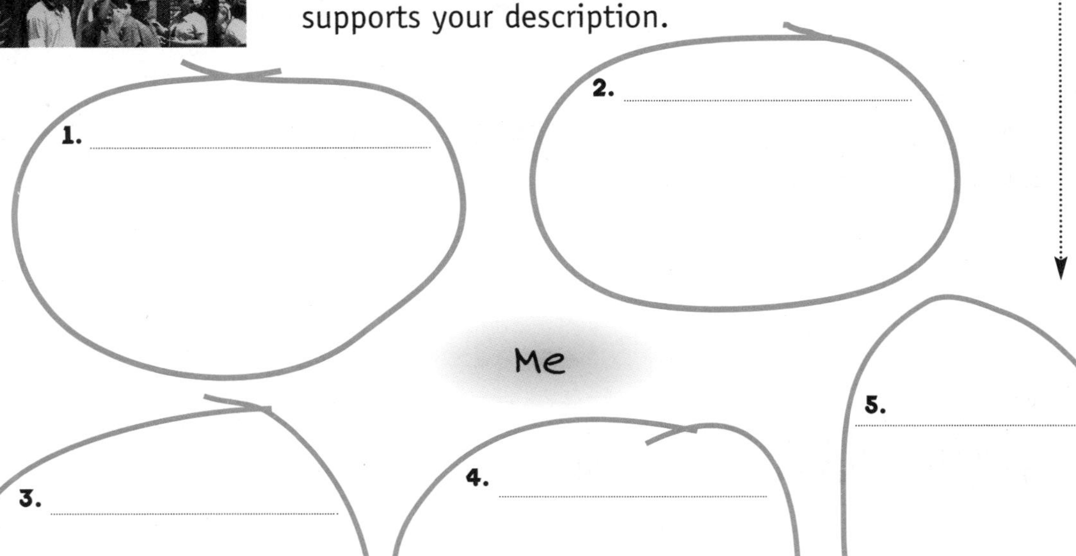

1. ______

2. ______

Me

3. ______

4. ______

5. ______

C. FOCUS Next prepare to write an autobiographical paragraph about 1 of the events you listed.

1. Be sure the event you write about will illustrate a particular personality trait.

2. Write an opening sentence that introduces the event.

EXAMPLE: WHEN I WAS 13, I TRIED OUT FOR THE BASKETBALL TEAM.

My opening sentence:

D. ADD DETAILS List details of what happened, why you acted the way you did, and what the experience shows about you.

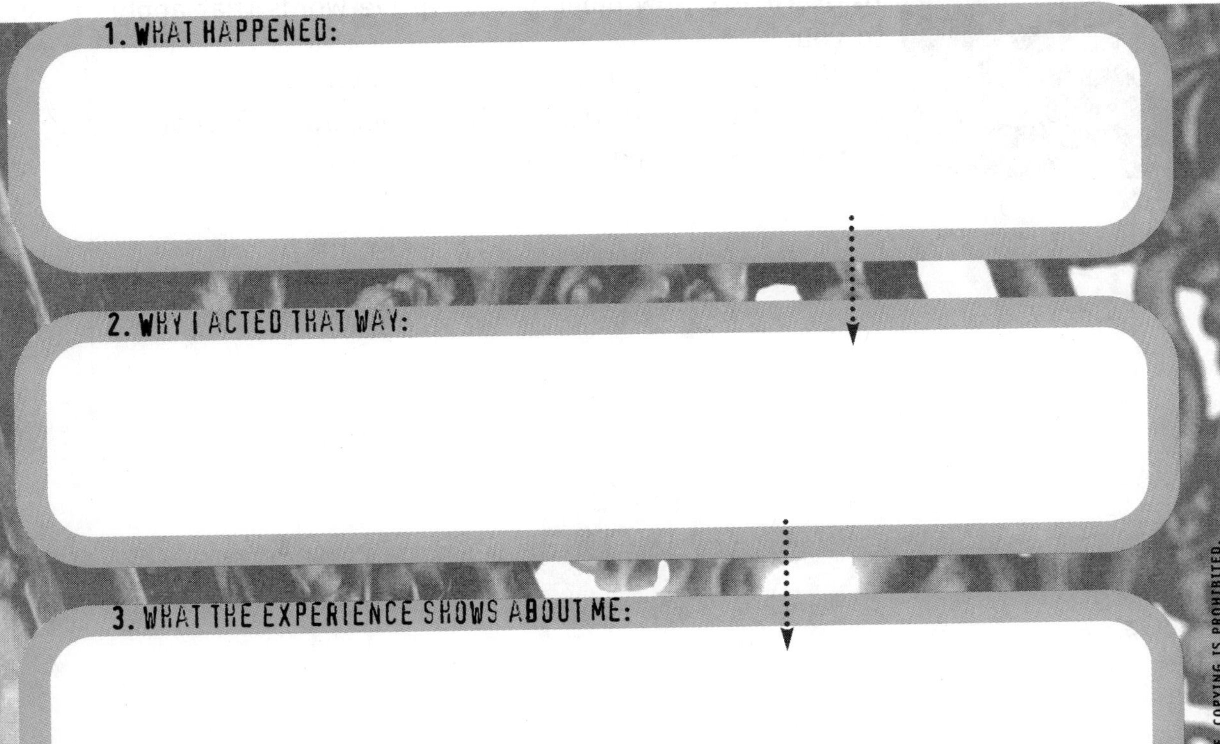

1. WHAT HAPPENED:
2. WHY I ACTED THAT WAY:
3. WHAT THE EXPERIENCE SHOWS ABOUT ME:

IV. WRITE

Now write an **autobiographical paragraph** about an incident in your life.

1. Begin with your topic sentence.
2. Tell what happened, why you acted the way you did, and what the event reveals about you.
3. Use the Writers' Checklist to help you revise.

Continue your writing on the next page.

WRITERS' CHECKLIST

CAPITALIZATION

- ❑ **Did you capitalize titles that come before proper nouns?** EXAMPLES: Dr. Chen, Mrs. Minnick, Captain Stein
- ❑ **Did you capitalize titles that describe family relationships, when they are used with or in place of a proper name?** EXAMPLES: I think Aunt Eloise and my mother saw the accident. Yesterday Father got an award.

Continue your writing from the previous page.

V. WRAP-UP

What did you like most about Victor Martinez's style of writing? What did you like least?

READERS' CHECKLIST

STYLE

- ☐ Did you find the passage well written?
- ☐ Are the sentences well constructed and the words well chosen?
- ☐ Does the style show you how to be a better writer?

18: Picking

Do you watch movie previews? A movie preview gives you a little taste of the movie before you actually see it. The same thing happens when you preview what you're about to read.

I. BEFORE YOU READ

What should you look for in a preview? Read the questions in the Preview Card below.

1. Then preview the selection "Picking" by glancing through it. Look for character names, key words, and art that will help you answer the questions.
2. Make notes in each box of the Preview Card below.

Preview Card

WHO ARE THE CHARACTERS?	WHAT ARE SOME KEY WORDS?
WHAT DOES THE ART REMIND YOU OF?	**WHAT'S THE STORY ABOUT?**

II. READ

Now read "Picking."

1. As you read, try to **predict** what will happen to Nardo next.
2. Use the Response Notes to write your predictions.

Response Notes

EXAMPLE: Nardo will lose another job.

"Picking" from *Parrot in the Oven*
by Victor Martinez

I wasn't like Nardo. I suppose years of not knowing what, besides work, was expected from a Mexican convinced me that I wouldn't pass from this earth without putting in a lot of days. I suppose Nardo figured the same, and wasn't about to waste his time. But I was of my grandpa Ignacio's line of useful blood. All his life, no matter what the job, my grandpa worked like a man trying to fill all his tomorrows with one solid day's work. Even in the end, when he got sick and couldn't move, he hated sitting on the couch doing nothing. He'd fumble around the house fixing sockets and floor trim, painting lower shelves and screwing legs back on to tables, although the finished chore was always more a sign of how much his mind had gotten older than anything else.

stop+clarify

What does the narrator mean when he says that he is of his grandfather's line of "useful blood"?

stop+clarify

VOCABULARY

sockets—electrical fixtures.
floor trim—bottom part of the wall that touches the floor.

"Picking" continued

Response Notes

For a while, I hustled fruit with my cousins Rio and Pete. Their dad, my uncle Joe, owned a panel truck, and together we sold melons, apples, oranges—whatever grew in season—from door to door. But when my uncle hurt his leg tripping over some tree roots, and his ankle swelled up blue and tender as a ripened plum and he couldn't walk, except maybe to hobble on one leg to the refrigerator or lean over to change channels on the TV, he took the panel truck away.

Without work, I was empty as a Coke bottle. School was starting soon, and I needed money for clothes and paper stuff. I wanted a baseball mitt so bad a sweet hurt blossomed in my stomach whenever I thought about it. Baseball had a grip on my fantasies then, and I couldn't shake it loose. There was an outfielder's glove in the window of Duran's Department Store that kept me dreaming downright dangerous outfield catches. I decided to stir up Nardo to see if he'd go pick chili peppers with me.

"You can buy more weights!" I said a bit too enthusiastically, making him suspicious right off the bat.

He looked up at me from the middle of a push-up. "You think I'm lazy, don't you?"

"No," I lied.

VOCABULARY

hustled—sold.
melons—large, sweet, juicy fruit such as watermelon that grow on vines.
hobble—walk awkwardly; limp.
blossomed—developed.
enthusiastically—excitedly.
suspicious—distrustful.

stop+summarize

What 3 things have you learned about the narrator?

1.

2.

3.

Response Notes

"Picking" continued

"Yeah, you do. You think I'm lazy," he said, breathing tight as he pushed off the floor.

"I said no!"

"Yeah, you do." He forced air into his lungs, then got up miserably wiping his hands.

"But that's all right, little boy, if you think I'm lazy. Everybody else does." He started picking at a sliver in his palm. "I'm not really lazy, you know. I've been working off and on." He greedily bit the sliver, moving his elbow up and down like a bird's wing. "If Mom wants me to go," he said, finally, "I'll go. If that's what she wants. But I'm telling you right now, if it gets hot I'm quitting."

Miracles don't wait for doubters, so the next morning I asked my dad if we could borrow his car, a Plymouth, which Nardo could drive despite the tricky gearshift. Dad was pretty cheery about me getting Nardo out of hibernation. He gave us some paint cans for the chili peppers and practically put a Christmas ribbon on the large brimmed hats

VOCABULARY

sliver—splinter.
Miracles—unexplainable, marvelous events.
tricky gearshift—problems with the stick shift.
hibernation—state of inactivity.

"Picking" continued

Response Notes

from Mexico he'd bought years ago. The headbands were already dark with sweat and the straw furry with dust, but they'd protect us from the sun.

stop+predict

What will happen when they go to the field to pick chilis?

stop+predict

When we arrived at the chili field, the wind through the window was warm on our shirtsleeves. Already the sky was beginning to hollow out, the clouds rushing toward the rim of the horizon as if even they knew the sun would soon be the center of a boiling pot.

The foreman, wearing a pale-yellow shirt with a black-leather vest and cowboy boots with curled tips, refused at first to hire us, saying I was too young, that it was too late in the day—most field workers got up at the first wink of dawn. Besides, all the rows had been taken hours ago. He laughed at the huge lunch bag bulging under Nardo's arm, and said we looked like two kids strolling out on a picnic.

Although he could fake disappointment better than anybody, deep down I believed

VOCABULARY

horizon—line along which the earth and sky appear to meet.
foreman—man in charge of the work crew.

Nardo wanted to give picking chilies a try. But a good excuse was a good excuse, and any excuse was better than quitting. So he hurriedly threw his can into the car trunk and made a stagy flourish with his hand before opening the side door.

stop+clarify

How did the foreman react to their request to work?

Seeing him so spunky, I thought it nothing less than torture when the foreman said that, fortunately for us, there was a scrawny row next to the road no one wanted. The foreman must have thought it a big joke, giving us that row. He chuckled and called us over with a sneaky offer of his arm, as if to share a secret.

"*Vamos, muchachos, aquí hay un surco muy bueno que pueden piscar*," he said, gesturing down at some limp branches leaning away from the road, as if trying to lift their roots and hustle away from the passing traffic. The leaves were sparse and shriveled, dying for air, and they had a coat of white pesticide dust and exhaust fumes so thick you could smear

VOCABULARY

stagy—theatrical.
spunky—spirited; lively.
scrawny—lean.
"Vamos, muchachos, aquí hay un surco muy bueno que pueden piscar."—Spanish for "Come on, guys, here is a very good area for picking."
sparse—thin.
white pesticide—chemicals sprayed on the plants to keep weeds down and to kill insects.

"Picking" continued

Response Notes

your hands on the leaves and rub fingerprints with them.

My brother shrugged. His luck gone, there was not much else he could do. The foreman hung around a bit to make sure we knew which peppers to pick and which to leave for the next growing, not that it mattered in that row.

We'd been picking about two hours when the sun began scalding the backs of our hands, leaving a pocket of heat, crawling like a small animal inside our shirts. My fingers were as rubbery as old carrots, and it seemed forever before the peppers rose to the center of my can. Nardo topped his can before I did, patted the chilies down and lifted it over his shoulder, his rock of an arm solid against his cheek.

"I'm gonna get my money and buy me a soda," he said, and strode off toward the weighing area, carefully swishing his legs between the plants. I limped behind him, straining with my half-filled can of lungless chili peppers.

VOCABULARY

scalding—burning.
rubbery—elastic; flexible.

stop+question

What does the narrator learn about himself and his brother?

GATHER YOUR THOUGHTS

A. REFLECT The brief stories that writers tell to help make a point or support an argument are called anecdotes.

What point is the narrator trying to make with the anecdote of what happened in the chili field?

B. PLAN AN ESSAY Now think about a time you worked hard—maybe at a challenging job or on a difficult school assignment.

1. Get ready to write an autobiographical essay that tells about that time.
2. Use the boxes below to plan what you will write in each of the 3 paragraphs of your essay.

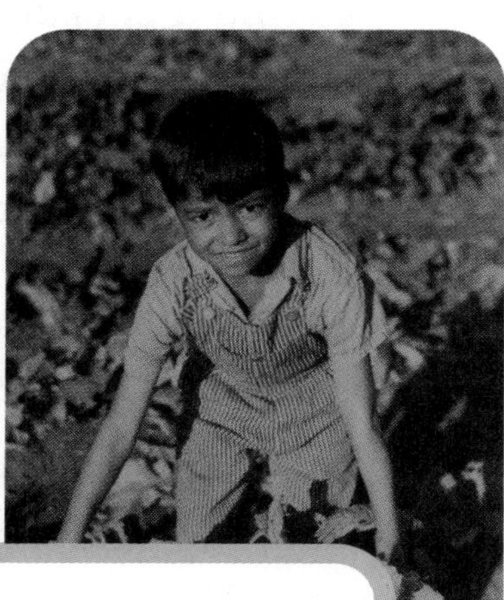

1st paragraph

INTRODUCTION (SET THE SCENE)

2nd paragraph

BODY (GIVE DETAILS OF THE EXPERIENCE)

3rd paragraph

CONCLUSION (EXPLAIN THE POINT OF WHAT YOU LEARNED FROM THE EXPERIENCE)

IV. WRITE

Now write an **autobiographical essay** about a time you worked hard.

1. Use the notes on the previous page to help you organize your writing into 3 paragraphs.
2. Use the Writers' Checklist to help you revise.

Continue your writing on the next page.

Continue your writing from the previous page.

WRITERS' CHECKLIST

COMMAS

- ❑ **Did you use commas to set off explanatory phrases?** EXAMPLE: *My dad's car, a green Honda, backfired.*
- ❑ **Did you use commas to set off introductory phrases?** EXAMPLE: *During June, my sister graduated from high school.*
- ❑ **Did you use commas to set off interruptions?** EXAMPLE: *It was, of course, the most exciting basketball game I've seen.*

WRAP-UP

What did reading "Picking" make you think about?

READERS' CHECKLIST

DEPTH

- ❑ **Did the reading make you think about things?**
- ❑ **Did it set off thoughts beyond the surface topic?**

Fitting In

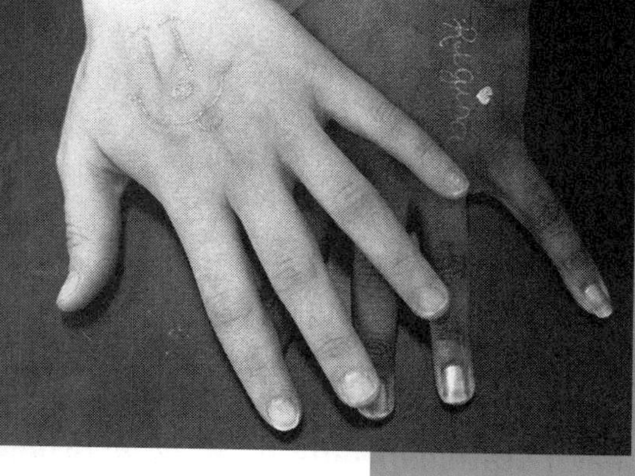

The world is a colorful mix of people from all backgrounds. Yet many people try to erase the traits that set them apart from others. Instead, they try to blend in and not call attention to themselves. People struggle in different ways to fit in, often without recognizing that the real issue is acceptance, self-confidence, or something else.

Would you start out on a journey without first checking a map? You probably wouldn't. Do the same preparation with your reading. Before you begin a story or article, try to get a sense of where it's going.

I. BEFORE YOU READ

With a partner, read each statement below. Circle whether you agree or disagree.

1. Discuss your answers with your reading partner.
2. After reading the selection, come back and look at each statement again. Mark whether you agree or disagree.

ANTICIPATION GUIDE

BEFORE READING agree	BEFORE READING disagree		AFTER READING agree	AFTER READING disagree
☐	☐	1. THE COLOR OF YOUR SKIN CAN AFFECT THE WAY PEOPLE TREAT YOU.	☐	☐
☐	☐	2. ALL PEOPLE ARE TREATED EQUALLY IN THE UNITED STATES.	☐	☐
☐	☐	3. EVERYONE IS A LITTLE BIT PREJUDICED.	☐	☐
☐	☐	4. HOW OTHERS FEEL ABOUT YOU IS MORE IMPORTANT THAN HOW YOU FEEL ABOUT YOURSELF.	☐	☐
☐	☐	5. ANYONE CAN BE INVISIBLE.	☐	☐
☐	☐	6. RACIAL PREJUDICE IS A FACT OF LIFE.	☐	☐

II. READ

Read "The Story of My Body."

1. As you read, pay attention to how Ortiz Cofer feels about herself.

2. List your **questions** about her feelings in the Response Notes.

"The Story of My Body" by Judith Ortiz Cofer

Migration is the story of my body.
—Víctor Hernández Cruz

SKIN

I was born a white girl in Puerto Rico but became a brown girl when I came to live in the United States. My Puerto Rican relatives called me tall; at the American school, some of my rougher classmates called me Skinny Bones, and the Shrimp because I was the smallest member of my classes all through grammar school until high school, when the midget Gladys was given the honorary post of front row center for class pictures and scorekeeper, bench warmer, in P.E. I reached my full stature of five feet in sixth grade.

I started out life as a pretty baby and learned to be a pretty girl from a pretty mother. Then at ten years of age I suffered one of the worst cases of chicken pox I have ever heard of. My entire body, including the inside of my ears and in-between my toes, was covered with pustules which in a fit of panic at my appearance I scratched off my face,

RESPONSE NOTES

EXAMPLE:
Did the teasing enbarrass her?

VOCABULARY

stature—height.
chicken pox—contagious virus marked by fever and blotches on the skin.
pustules—blisters filled with pus.

RESPONSE NOTES

leaving permanent scars. A cruel school nurse told me I would always have them—tiny cuts that looked as if a mad cat had plunged its claws deep into my skin. I grew my hair long and hid behind it for the first years of my adolescence. This was when I learned to be invisible.

STOP AND THINK

Why does she make herself invisible?

Have you ever felt the same way? Explain why.

COLOR

In the animal world it indicates danger: the most colorful creatures are often the most poisonous. Color is also a way to attract and seduce a mate. In the human world color triggers many more complex and often deadly reactions. As a Puerto Rican girl born of "white" parents, I spent the first years of my life hearing people refer to me as *blanca*, white. My mother insisted that I protect myself from the intense island sun because I was more prone to sunburn than some of my darker, *trigueño* playmates. People were always commenting within my hearing about how my black hair contrasted so nicely with

VOCABULARY

seduce—attract.
trigueño—olive-skinned.

RESPONSE NOTES

my "pale" skin. I did not think of the color of my skin consciously except when I heard the adults talking about complexion. It seems to me that the subject is much more common in the conversation of mixed-race peoples than in mainstream United States society, where it is a touchy and sometimes even embarrassing topic to discuss, except in a political context. In Puerto Rico I heard many conversations about skin color. A pregnant woman could say, "I hope my baby doesn't turn out *prieto*" (slang for "dark" or "black") "like my husband's grandmother, although she was a good-looking *negra* in her time." I am a combination of both, being olive-skinned—lighter than my mother yet darker than my fair-skinned father. In America, I am a person of color, obviously a Latina. On the Island I have been called everything from a *paloma blanca*, after the song (by a black suitor), to *la gringa*.

STOP AND THINK

Why is skin color so important to her family and friends?

My first experience of color prejudice occurred in a supermarket in Paterson, New

VOCABULARY

complexion—skin color.
mainstream—the major part of.
paloma blanca—Spanish for "white dove."
la gringa—Spanish for "the foreigner."

RESPONSE NOTES

Jersey. It was Christmastime, and I was eight or nine years old. There was a display of toys in the store where I went two or three times a day to buy things for my mother, who never made lists but sent for milk, cigarettes, a can of this or that, as she remembered from hour to hour. I enjoyed being trusted with money and walking half a city block to the new, modern grocery store. It was owned by three good-looking Italian brothers. I liked the younger one with the crew-cut blond hair. The two older ones watched me and the other Puerto Rican kids as if they thought we were going to steal something. The oldest one would sometimes even try to hurry me with my purchases, although part of my pleasure in these expeditions came from looking at everything in the well-stocked aisles. I was also teaching myself to read English by sounding out the labels in packages: L&M cigarettes, Borden's homogenized milk, Red Devil potted ham, Nestle's chocolate mix, Quaker oats, Bustelo coffee, Wonder bread, Colgate toothpaste, Ivory Soap, and Goya (makers of products used in Puerto Rican dishes) everything—these are some of the brand names that taught me nouns.

VOCABULARY

expeditions—outings.
aisles—rows.
homogenized milk—milk in which the fat is mixed throughout so that it does not rise to the top of the bottle, as it does with cream.

STOP AND THINK

Why does she like the grocery story so much?

STOP AND THINK

RESPONSE NOTES

Several times this man had come up to me, wearing his blood-stained butcher's apron, and towering over me had asked in a harsh voice whether there was something he could help me find. On the way out I would glance at the younger brother who ran one of the registers and he would often smile and wink at me.

It was the mean brother who first referred to me as "colored." It was a few days before Christmas, and my parents had already told my brother and me that since we were in Los Estados now, we would get our presents on December 25 instead of *Los Reyes,* Three Kings Day, when gifts are exchanged in Puerto Rico. We were to give them a wish list that they would take to Santa Claus, who apparently lived in the Macy's store downtown—at least that's where we had caught a glimpse of him when we went shopping. Since my parents were timid about entering the fancy store, we did not approach the huge man in the red suit. I was not interested in sitting on a stranger's lap anyway, but I did covet Susie, the talking schoolteacher doll that was displayed in the center aisle of the Italian brothers' supermarket.

VOCABULARY

Los Estados—Spanish for "the States," specifically the United Sates.
covet—desire; want.

RESPONSE NOTES

She talked when you pulled a string on her back. Susie had a limited repertoire of three sentences: I think she could say: "Hello, I'm Susie Schoolteacher," "Two plus two is four," and one other thing I cannot remember. The day the older brother chased me away, I was reaching to touch Susie's blonde curls. I had been told many times, as most children have, not to touch anything in a store that I was not buying, but I had been looking at Susie for weeks. In my mind, she was my doll. After all, I had put her on my Christmas wish list. The moment is frozen in my mind as if there were a photograph of it on file. It was not a turning point, a disaster, or an earthshaking revelation. It was simply the first time I considered—if naively—the meaning of skin color in human relations.

STOP AND THINK

Why do you think this doll is important to her?

I reached to touch Susie's hair. It seems to me that I had to get on tiptoe, since the toys were stacked on a table and she sat like a princess on top of the fancy box she came in. Then I heard the booming "Hey, kid, what do

VOCABULARY

repertoire—collection.
revelation—understanding.
naively—innocently.

"The Story of My Body" continued

RESPONSE NOTES

you think you're doing!" spoken very loudly from the meat counter. I felt caught, although I knew I was not doing anything criminal. I remember not looking at the man, but standing there, feeling humiliated because I knew everyone in the store must have heard him yell at me. I felt him approach, and when I knew he was behind me, I turned around to face the bloody butcher's apron. His large chest was at my eye level. He blocked my way. I started to run out of the place, but even as I reached the door I heard him shout after me: "Don't come in here unless you gonna buy something. You PR kids put your dirty hands on stuff. You always look dirty. But maybe dirty brown is your natural color." I heard him laugh and someone else too in the back.

STOP AND THINK

How does she feel about the man in the butcher's apron?

How do you feel about him?

Outside in the sunlight I looked at my hands. My nails needed a little cleaning as they always did, since I liked to paint with watercolors, but I took a bath every night. I

VOCABULARY

humiliated—ashamed or without a sense of self-respect.

RESPONSE NOTES

thought the man was dirtier than I was in his stained apron. He was also always sweaty—it showed in big yellow circles under his shirtsleeves. I sat on the front steps of the apartment building where we lived and looked closely at my hands, which showed the only skin I could see, since it was bitter cold and I was wearing my quilted play coat, dungarees, and a knitted navy cap of my father's. I was not pink like my friend Charlene and her sister Kathy, who had blue eyes and light brown hair. My skin is the color of the coffee my grandmother made, which was half milk, *leche con café* rather than *café con leche*. My mother is the opposite mix. She has a lot of café in her color. I could not understand how my skin looked like dirt to the supermarket man.

I went in and washed my hands thoroughly with soap and hot water, and borrowing my mother's nail file, I cleaned the crusted watercolors from underneath my nails. I was pleased with the results. My skin was the same color as before, but I knew I was clean. Clean enough to run my fingers through Susie's fine gold hair when she came home to me.

VOCABULARY

dungarees—jeans.

Now return to your Anticipation Guide on page 184. Complete the "After Reading" column. Have you changed your mind about any of the statements?

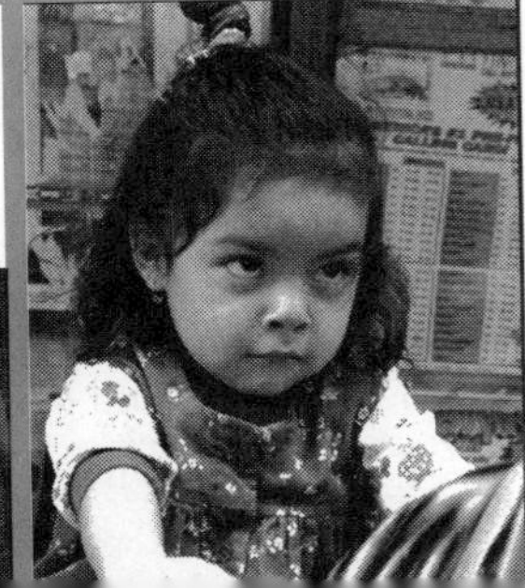

III. GATHER YOUR THOUGHTS

A. REFLECT Think about the similarities and differences between how Ortiz Cofer sees herself and how others view her. Complete the Venn diagram to clarify your thoughts.

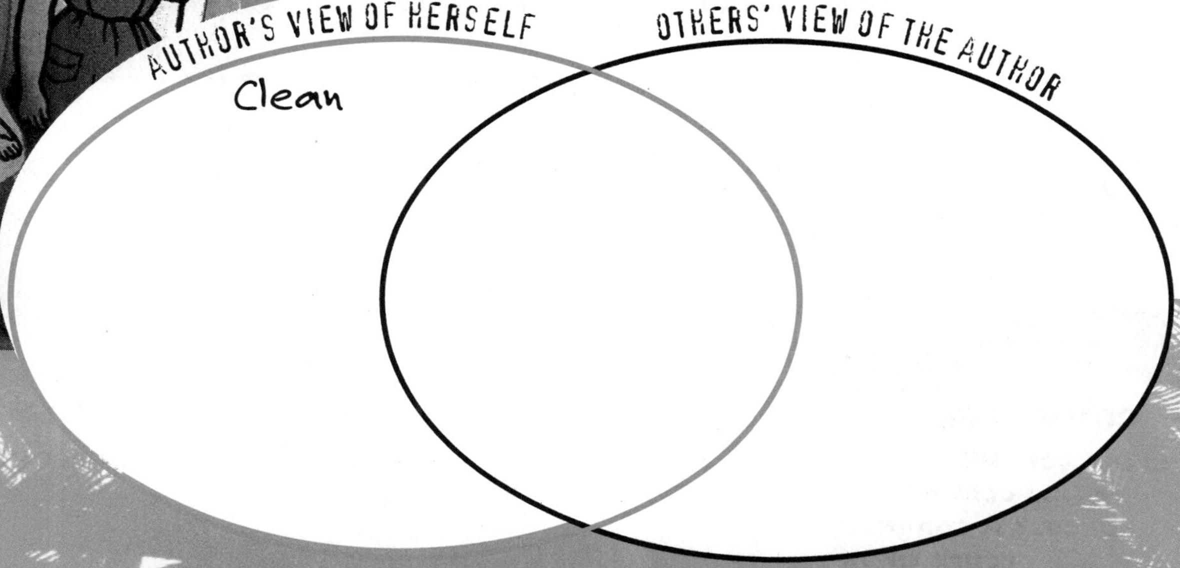

AUTHOR'S VIEW OF HERSELF

Clean

OTHERS' VIEW OF THE AUTHOR

B. SUPPORT AN OPINION In "The Story of My Body," Judith Ortiz Cofer writes about the image she had of herself. Get ready to write a paragraph in which you explain your opinion of the following statement:

How others see you is not as important as how you see yourself.

1. Decide whether you agree or disagree with the statement.
2. List below 3 reasons or examples that help explain why you feel the way you do.

(circle one)

I agree / disagree that how others see you is not as important as how you see yourself.

1.

2.

3.

WRITE

Write a **paragraph of opinion.** Use your notes to help you make clear whether or not you agree with the statement about self-image.

1. Include at least 3 reasons for your opinion.
2. Use the Writers' Checklist to help you revise.

WRITERS' CHECKLIST

COMMA SPLICES

- [ ] **Did you avoid writing comma splices? A comma splice occurs when two simple sentences are joined with just a comma. Incorrect:** ***She walked into the store, she touched the doll.*** **To fix a comma splice, you may need to add a conjunction (such as <u>and</u>, <u>or</u>, <u>but</u>, or <u>so</u>) before the comma. You may also replace the comma with a semicolon or create two separate sentences.** EXAMPLES: ***She walked into the store; she touched the doll. She walked into the store. She touched the doll.***

V. WRAP-UP

What did Judith Ortiz Cofer's "The Story of My Body" mean to you?

READERS' CHECKLIST

MEANING

- ❑ **Did you learn something from the reading?**
- ❑ **Did it affect you or make an impression?**

What does a poem mean? Poets write poetry for any number of reasons—to express feelings and emotions, to explore ideas, to "say" something to the world. But when you read a poem, look first at what it says to you.

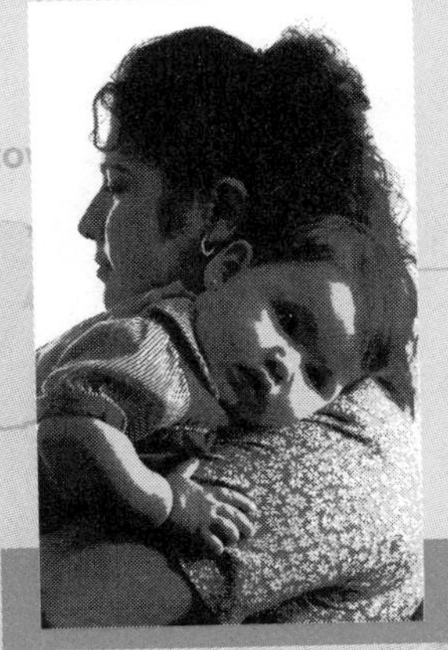

I. BEFORE YOU READ

Think about the title of the poem, "Child of the Americas," by Aurora Levins Morales. What does the title suggest to you?

1. Use the Word Web below to explore the meaning of the words in the poem's title.
2. Write 5 or 6 thoughts about what the poem might be about.

WORD WEB

"Child of the Americas"

II. READ

As you read "Child of the Americas," think about how the poem makes you feel.

1. **React** and **connect** to particular lines by jotting down your ideas in the Response Notes.
2. Describe how the lines relate to or remind you of your own feelings and experiences.

"Child of the Americas"

by Aurora Levins Morales

I am a child of the Americas,
a light-skinned mestiza of the Caribbean,
a child of many diaspora, born into this
continent at a crossroads.

I am a U.S. Puerto Rican Jew,
a product of the ghettos of New York I have
never known.
An immigrant and the daughter and
granddaughter of immigrants.
I speak English with passion: it's the tongue
of my consciousness,
a flashing knife blade of crystal, my tool,
my craft.

I am Caribeña, island grown. Spanish is in
my flesh,
ripples from my tongue, lodges in my hips:
the language of garlic and mangoes,
the singing in my poetry, the flying gestures
of my hands.

RESPONSE NOTES

EXAMPLE:
I don't even know where my grandparents are from.

VOCABULARY

mestiza—female of European and Native-American ancestry.
diaspora—cultures.
ghettos—sections of a city where many minority groups live.
mangoes—tropical fruit.

RESPONSE NOTES

I am of Latinoamerica, rooted in the history
of my continent:
I speak from that body.

I am not african. Africa is in me, but I
cannot return.
I am not taína. Taíno is in me, but there is
no way back.
I am not European. Europe lives in me, but I
have no home there.

I am new. History made me. My first
language was spanglish.
I was born at the crossroads
and I am whole.

VOCABULARY

taína—Native American, specifically member of the Arawak tribe of people who died out during the 16th century.
spanglish—mix of Spanish and English.

DOUBLE-ENTRY JOURNAL

Write 2 quotes from Morales's poem that seem interesting or important to you. Then explain how these lines make you feel.

QUOTES	MY THOUGHTS
1.	
2.	

III. GATHER YOUR THOUGHTS

A. FIND SENSORY DETAILS Most poems contain many sensory details. They come from the senses *(smell, touch, taste, hearing,* and *sight)*.

1. With a reading partner, reread the poem.
2. Complete the chart below, making a list of 3 sensory words or phrases you and your partner find.

"CHILD OF THE AMERICAS"

DETAIL	COMES FROM THE SENSE OF . . .
EXAMPLE: "the language of garlic and mangoes"	taste or smell
1.	
2.	
3.	

B. DEVELOP AN IDEA Get ready to write a poem of your own about an object that is important to you.

1. First list in the left column 3 objects that are special to you.
2. Next write how each object looks, smells, or feels.
3. Then write what each object means or says about you.

OBJECT	SENSORY WORDS	WHAT IT MEANS TO ME
1.	1.	1.
2.	2.	2.
3.	3.	3.

IV. WRITE

Now write a **poem** about one of the objects you wrote about on the previous page.

1. Make your poem at least 4 lines long.
2. Use several of the sensory words from your chart.
3. Use the Writers' Checklist to help you revise.

WRITERS' CHECKLIST

PLURAL NOUNS

- ❑ **Did you use the correct form of plural nouns? Most plural nouns are formed by adding *-s* to the singular form.** EXAMPLES: *cooks, dogs, girls*
  Add -es to form the plural of nouns that end in *ch, sh, x, z, s,* or *ss.* EXAMPLES: *churches, boxes, glasses*
  To form the plural of nouns that end in a consonant and *y*, change the *y* to *i* and add *-es* to form the plural. EXAMPLES: *libraries, cities, spies*

V. WRAP-UP

What, in your own words, is Aurora Levins Morales saying in "Child of the Americas"?

READERS' CHECKLIST

UNDERSTANDING

- ❑ **Did you understand the reading?**
- ❑ **Was the message or point clear?**
- ❑ **Can you restate what the reading is about?**

John F. Kennedy

Hitler reviewing his troops

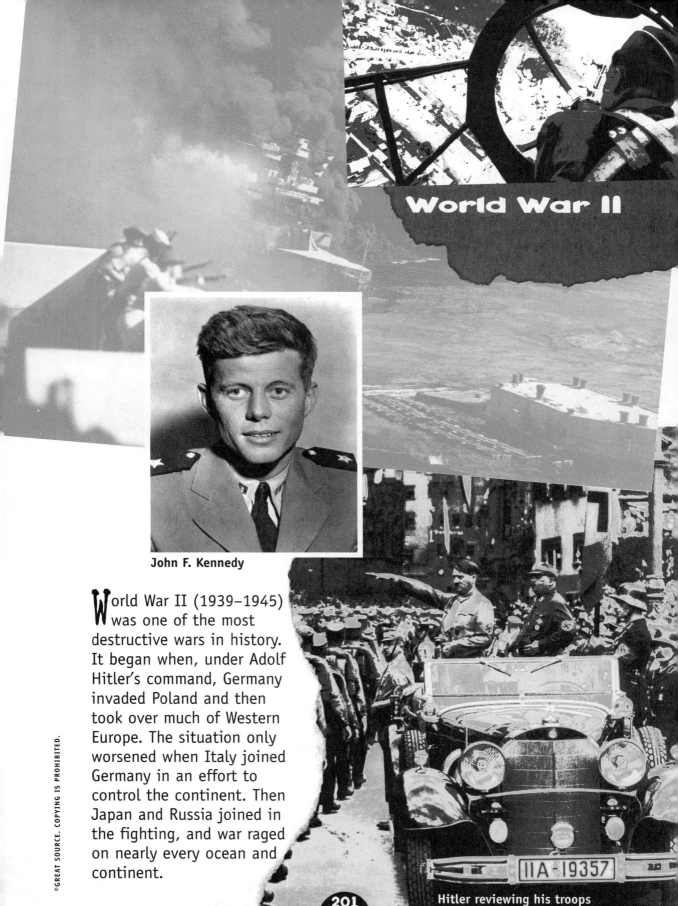

World War II (1939–1945) was one of the most destructive wars in history. It began when, under Adolf Hitler's command, Germany invaded Poland and then took over much of Western Europe. The situation only worsened when Italy joined Germany in an effort to control the continent. Then Japan and Russia joined in the fighting, and war raged on nearly every ocean and continent.

21: The War Arrives

What have you heard about World War II? What pictures or images of it come to mind? Most of us need to build some background before we read. Take a moment before you begin reading a book or article to look at any photos, maps, graphics, or other images.

I. BEFORE YOU READ

Take a Picture Walk through the selection.

1. Look carefully at each photo and read any captions.
2. Record some of your thoughts about 2 or 3 of the photos in this selection.
3. Make a prediction about the content of "The War Arrives."

A young refugee of the war in Europe

PICTURE WALK

THE PICTURE OF . . .	MAKES ME FEEL . . .
1.	
2.	
3.	

I predict this selection will be about:

II. READ

Now read "The War Arrives," part of a novel called *The Upstairs Room*.

1. **Mark** or **highlight** any details about the characters that you find surprising or interesting.
2. Write your ideas in the Response Notes.

Adolph Hitler

"The War Arrives" from *The Upstairs Room*
by Johanna Reiss

RESPONSE NOTES

A few months later Uncle Bram and his wife left for America. We went to the station to say good-bye. They must have been planning to stay for a long time. They took a lot of suitcases with them. And it must be far away, for Uncle Bram said that Hitler would never be able to reach them in America.

EXAMPLE: Narrator must be young to think this.

"Sophie, why don't we go too?" Father said.

But Mother said she had too many headaches to leave Holland and start all over again. Waving, we remained at the station until the train went. With angry steps Father walked over to his car, opened it, and got in. He slammed the door and drove away, leaving us to walk home.

By the fall of 1939, Rachel had graduated from teachers' college. She found a job at one of the nursery schools in Winterswijk. Sini started to work on a farm. At night when Father and Mother went across the street to sit outside with the Gans family, Mother tried to talk about my sisters. "That Rachel . . . so capable . . . and Sini, studying for her milking diploma. . . ." But I could tell from my window that nobody was

VOCABULARY

Hitler—founder of the German Nazi Party who ruled as a dictator during World War II.
Winterswijk—city in Poland.

RESPONSE NOTES

listening to her. They were talking about the Germans who had invaded Poland.

That was a bad thing to have done, Rachel told me. So bad that England and France had said to Germany, "Get your soldiers out of Poland, or else." But Hitler had just laughed, and now England and France were at war with Germany. Served him right.

STOP AND PREDICT

What do you think the family will do?

Why did I have to go to bed so early? It was still light out. After all, I was in second grade now. Tomorrow I would refuse to do it. I stuck my head farther out the window. Nobody looked up to tell me that I had to go back to bed, not even Mrs. Gans. They were too busy talking.

That winter the Gans family spent almost every night at our house, in front of the radio. They didn't have one of their own. Hitler did not seem to like Polish Jews either. He seemed to like them even less than German Jews. He had had some of them beaten so hard they had died, and they hadn't even done anything. How did he dare? I was often glad when Mother told me that it was time for me to go to bed. Under the blankets I couldn't hear the radio.

German soldiers marching into Holland

"The War Arrives" CONTINUED

"Sophie," Father said, "we can't stay here any longer. We must go to America, I just heard that the German army is in Denmark and Norway. Sophie, that's close! Do you hear me? We have no choice. We're Jews!"

"Ies, you know I don't feel well. How can I leave? You're shouting so my head hurts even more. Annie, go to the kitchen and play there."

Unwillingly I left. Why did Mother always have to have headaches?

RESPONSE NOTES

STOP AND THINK

Will Ies leave for America without his family? Explain your prediction.

Father started to build a house outside of Winterswijk, where Mother felt we would be about as safe as in America. It made Father furious to hear her say that. But he built the house anyway. The house wasn't going to be near that border. No, it would be far away, on the other side of Winterswijk. The Germans would not bother us there.

And then it was May 10, 1940. In the middle of the night I woke up. So much noise. I jumped out of bed. Where was everybody? They were on their way downstairs. I ran downstairs, too.

"What's happening?" I asked. "I hear planes. What are they going to do?"

Rotterdam, a city in Holland

STOP AND PREDICT

What do you think is happening?

RESPONSE NOTES

"The War Arrives" CONTINUED

"I'm sure they're German planes," Rachel said.

"Maybe there's war here, too," Sini said.

"This is it," Father mumbled. "Now it's our turn."

"How do you know they're German planes?" Mother asked.

"They're coming from the east. Can't you hear?" Father snapped.

The border was to the east. Why wasn't the new house ready? We'd be safe there. Mother had said so.

Father turned on the radio. The doorbell rang, and the Gans family stormed in. "What does the radio say?" "War, isn't it? We knew it."

German tanks occupying a European city

People lining up at a butcher shop for their rations of one ounce of meat

III. GATHER YOUR THOUGHTS

A. UNDERSTAND CHARACTERS Use the organizer below to explore the characters in "The War Arrives." Write 2 or 3 descriptive words or phrases about each character.

"The War Arrives"

Annie ("I")

Father ("Ies")

Mother ("Sophie")

B. DEVELOP DETAILS Get ready to write a character sketch about someone you know. Answer the questions below to develop details about the person.

1. What does he or she look like?

2. How old is he or she?

3. How does he or she dress?

4. What does the person like to do?

Person:

5. What does he or she not like?

6. What kind of person is he or she?

7. What does he or she talk about?

C. CONNECT DETAILS Now arrange the details about the person.

1. Look closely at the example below.
2. Use your notes to help you write a sentence that summarizes what the person is like.
3. Then write 3 details that support your impression of the person.

A building destroyed during the German invasion

EXAMPLE:

My aunt Esther is the most fascinating person I've ever met.

She loves to travel and has seen most of the world.	She wears exotic clothes that she's brought home from her adventures.	She teaches us games and jokes from other countries. She tells stories about her trips that keep me on the edge of my seat.

Your topic sentence:

DETAIL:

DETAIL:

DETAIL:

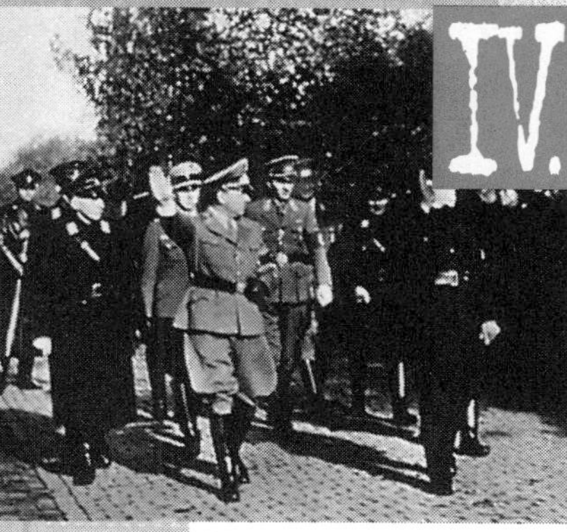

German soldiers marching into Holland

IV. WRITE

Write a **character sketch** of the person you chose.

1. Start with a topic sentence that summarizes your impression of the person.
2. Then give at least 3 details that support your impression.
3. Use the Writers' Checklist to help you revise.

Continue your writing on the next page.

WRITERS' CHECKLIST

ADJECTIVES

- ❑ **Did you use the correct (comparative) form to compare two things?** EXAMPLE: ***Of both of my brothers, John is taller.*** **(not the tallest)**
- ❑ **Did you use the correct (superlative) form to compare three or more things?** EXAMPLE: ***The assignments Mrs. Burt gives are the most unusual of those given by the other teachers in the school.*** **(not more unusual than)**

Continue your writing from the previous page.

V. WRAP-UP

What did you like or dislike about Reiss's style of writing?

READERS' CHECKLIST

STYLE

- ❑ **Did you find the passage well written?**
- ❑ **Are the sentences well constructed and the words well chosen?**
- ❑ **Does the style show you how to be a better writer?**

22: Disaster at Sea

How do you react to a crisis? Do you stay calm and cool, or do you panic? As you read the following excerpt of a biography about John F. Kennedy, you'll see how Kennedy reacted to the danger of an enemy ship during World War II.

I. BEFORE YOU READ

Before you read, help yourself understand and connect to the selection by thinking about anything you might have heard or read about John F. Kennedy.

1. In the **K** section, write notes about what you already know about Kennedy.
2. In the **W** section, write questions about Kennedy that you'd like answered. Save the **L** section for later.

K-W-L CHART

What I Know

What I Want to Know

What I Learned

II. READ

Now read this selection from *John F. Kennedy and PT-109.*

1. Write any **questions** you'd like to ask the author in the Response Notes.
2. Also jot down answers to your questions.

RESPONSE NOTES

EXAMPLE:
How many men were on each boat?

"Disaster at Sea" by Richard Tregaskis

It seemed to Lieutenant Kennedy on 109 and Lieutenant Lowrey on 162 that they had missed all the excitement. Both officers knew from the white flashes and heavy cannonading that ship action had been joined. But their own boats had been too far to the north.

As ordered, they kept on patrolling at slow speed. Only one engine on each boat was in gear in order to keep down the wake. Thus the boats would be less visible to the pesky Japanese float planes in the clouds.

From the babble on the short-wave radio, Kennedy couldn't tell what had happened. Had the PTs sunk the enemy or perhaps turned him back? Or had the destroyers slipped through Blackett Strait and—if so—would they be making their exit on the other side of Kolombangara through Kula Gulf? Or was it possible they had reached their destination and might be coming back through Blackett Strait?

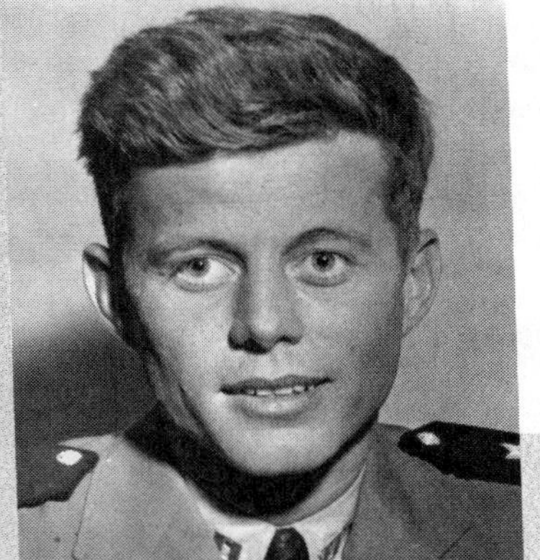

VOCABULARY

109—Kennedy's boat was called a PT-109, a fast patrol boat.
cannonading—firing.
wake—visible track of rough water created by the boat's movement.
babble—confusing talk.
PTs—fast boats used to patrol and torpedo enemy shipping. They were used extensively in the South Pacific during World War II.
destroyers—huge warships.
destination—place people are going.

Any one of those four possibilities could have occurred. Or more enemy forces—cruisers, destroyers, landing barges, planes—might be coming behind them. One thing Lieutenant Kennedy could be sure of: He had been involved in the kind of big engagement he longed for, and still had not fired a shot.

Time was passing, with no fresh gunfire flashes, new flares or thunder from destroyer batteries. The night was quiet. At 2:00 A.M., the boats were creeping up Blackett Strait, having been joined by PT-169, a stray from another division. PT-157 was also nearby, though she had not been in contact with them.

Just about 2:30 A.M., as the boats were edging along in the still, black waters, a lookout in Kennedy's boat suddenly cried out: "Ship at two o'clock!"

The ship was the looming, towering shape of the destroyer *Amagiri*, bearing directly down upon Kennedy and his crew. (The force of four Japanese destroyers was steaming back in a column from a successful supply drop at Vila.)

Kennedy and Radioman Maguire, standing side-by-side in the cockpit, saw the loom of the destroyer over them. Maguire heard Kennedy yell: "Hey—look at this!"

The young skipper hit Maguire on the arm and ordered, "Sound general quarters!"

RESPONSE NOTES

VOCABULARY

cruisers—fast warships.
landing barges—freight boats.
looming—massive; threatening.
bearing—coming.

Use a graphic organizer to keep track of the sequence of events. Write 3 things that have happened so far.

STOP & ORGANIZE

1.	2.	3.

"Disaster at Sea" CONTINUED

RESPONSE NOTES

Maguire shouted: "General quarters! General quarters!" while Kennedy hit the engine-room telegraph lever signaling engines full ahead. He flung the wheel over hard to the right. The bow of the destroyer was looming ahead now like a charging skyscraper. But instead of turning away from the enemy, Kennedy was trying to line up his boat for a torpedo shot, risking it even at such close range. Before he could bring his range estimators to bear, Kennedy saw with alarm that the PT was responding very sluggishly, failing to turn.

Up on the bow, where Starkey and other crew members had rigged the old 37-millimeter fieldpiece, "Barney" Ross was trying valiantly to get the gun into action against the destroyer. He fumbled with a shell, attempting to shove it into the breech.

At that moment, the looming steel shape crashed into the boat with crushing force, charging diagonally into the right side and

VOCABULARY

torpedo shot—chance to fire his underwater-moving weapon.
estimators—devices that calculate position.
37-millimeter fieldpiece—weapon.
valiantly—bravely.
breech—part behind the weapon's barrel.

knocking Kennedy and Maguire flat onto the cockpit deck. The destroyer severed the boat into two angular pieces, chopping off a section which included the starboard engine. Kennedy, flat on his back, saw above him the raked gray stacks of the Japanese destroyer, illuminated by an orange flash. There were the funnels with the upside-down Y-shape he had studied so many times in recognition courses.

Below decks, gasoline exploded around the engine, searing Engineer McMahon on the face and hands as he was knocked against the starboard bulkhead. At practically the same instant, he was flooded by salt water as the rear corner of the boat began to sink, gasoline still burning on the water.

RESPONSE NOTES

Write 3 more things that happened next.

STOP & ORGANIZE

4.

5.

6.

Starkey, who had jumped for his battle station beside the after starboard torpedo, had

VOCABULARY

severed—split; cut.
angular—angled.
starboard—on the right-hand side.
illuminated—lightened; made bright.
funnels—cone-shaped smokestacks.
searing—burning.
starboard bulkhead—upright structure on the right-hand side of a ship that prevents the spread of leakage or fire.

RESPONSE NOTES

fallen into the sinking, flaming engine compartment on the port side.

Johnston, another engineer, had been asleep on deck when Maguire gave the general quarters alarm. He saw the flash, the stack of the destroyer passing, and then was suddenly overboard, being turned end over end in the water by the rotating movement of the destroyer's propeller.

Kennedy struggled to his feet in the cockpit and saw and heard the gasoline burning on the water. His half of the boat was afloat, kept up by watertight compartments, which were undamaged. Maguire, Mauer and Albert, at least, were still aboard with him.

Gasoline, from the part of the boat which had sunk, was burning on the water only a few feet away. Kennedy was afraid the flames might reach the floating section of the hull, so he ordered the crewmen into the water. But the flames moved the other way, and the men climbed back aboard.

VOCABULARY

compartment—room.
rotating—circular.

Write 3 more events from Kennedy's story.

STOP & ORGANIZE

7.

8.

9.

Return to the K-W-L Chart on page 211 and fill in the **L** space.

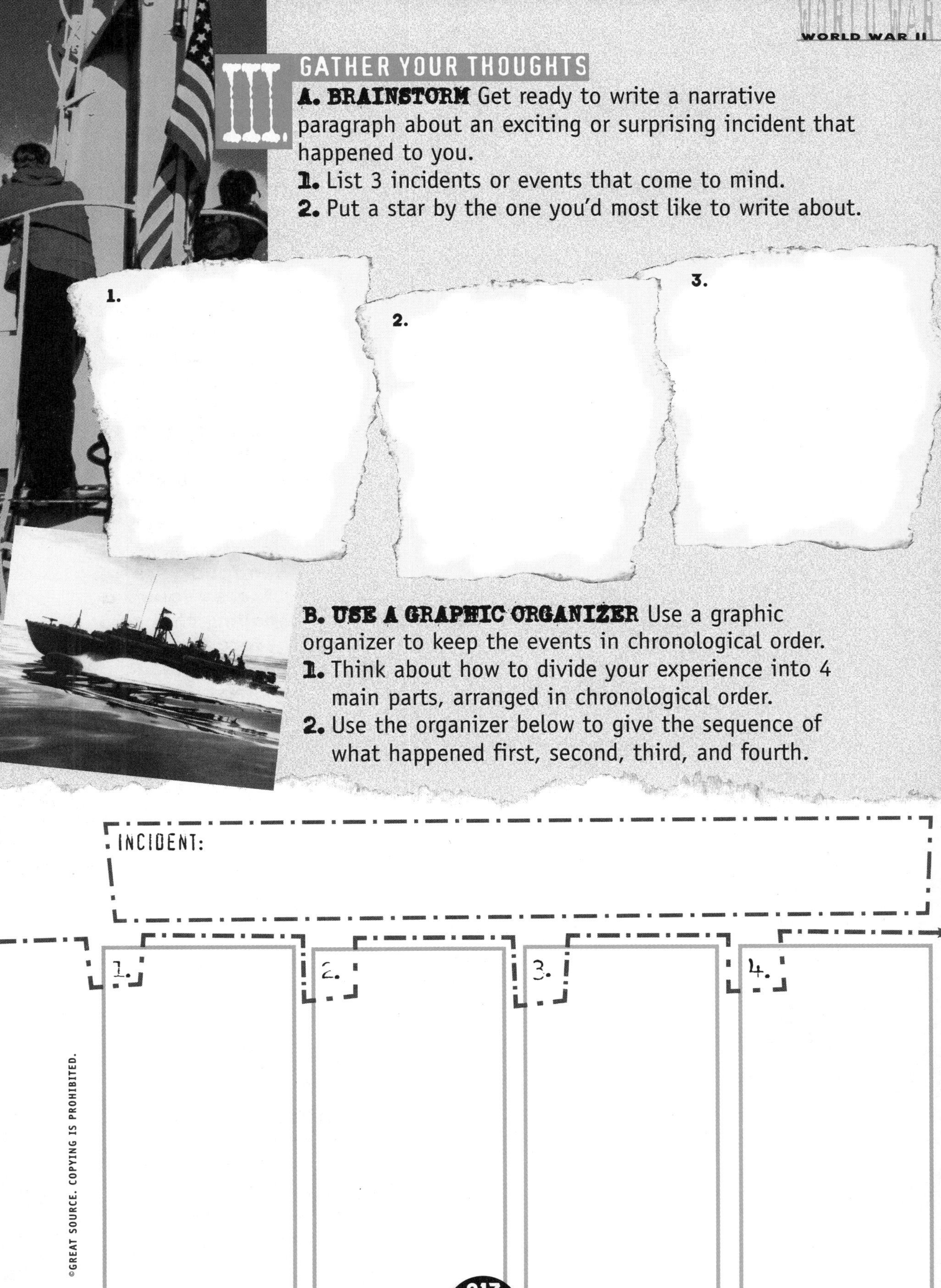

III. GATHER YOUR THOUGHTS

A. BRAINSTORM Get ready to write a narrative paragraph about an exciting or surprising incident that happened to you.

1. List 3 incidents or events that come to mind.
2. Put a star by the one you'd most like to write about.

1.

2.

3.

B. USE A GRAPHIC ORGANIZER Use a graphic organizer to keep the events in chronological order.

1. Think about how to divide your experience into 4 main parts, arranged in chronological order.
2. Use the organizer below to give the sequence of what happened first, second, third, and fourth.

INCIDENT:

1.

2.

3.

4.

IV. WRITE

Now write a **narrative paragraph** telling about an exciting or surprising incident.

1. Use chronological order to give details about how the experience unfolded.
2. Use the Writers' Checklist to help you revise.

WRITERS' CHECKLIST

PLURALS

- ❑ **Did you check that all plural forms are spelled correctly? Change *f* or *fe* to *v* and add *-es* to form the plural of most nouns ending in *f* or *fe*.** EXAMPLES: ***halves, wives, shelves***
  Some nouns are spelled the same in their singular and plural forms. EXAMPLES: ***sheep, deer, scissors, headquarters***
  Others require a spelling change before they can become plural. EXAMPLES: ***woman/women, man/men, goose/geese***

V. WRAP-UP

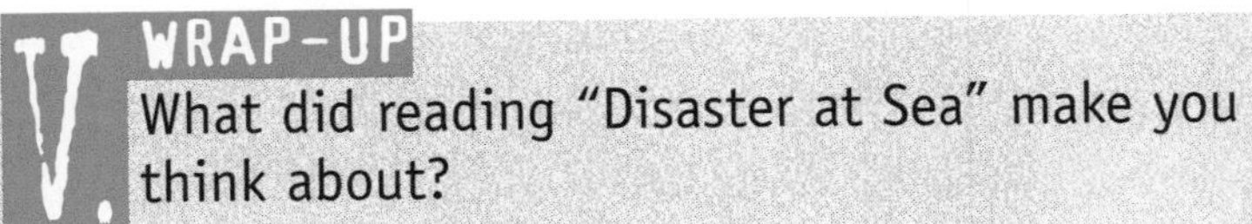

What did reading "Disaster at Sea" make you think about?

READERS' CHECKLIST

DEPTH

- ❑ **Did the reading make you think about things?**
- ❑ **Did it set off thoughts beyond the surface topic?**

Christopher Paul Curtis

Christopher Paul Curtis was born in Flint, Michigan, where he spent his first 13 years out of high school working on an assembly line in a factory. He later attended college and launched what has become a highly successful writing career. In 2000, Curtis won the two highest awards in children's literature—the Newbery Medal and the Coretta Scott King Award—for his novel *Bud, Not Buddy*.

23: Super-duper-cold Saturdays

Have you ever heard people say "first impressions are everything"? Many writers believe this is true. They spend a long time revising and editing their sentences, making sure they have used just the right words. They want to create the right mood so that it's easy for readers to become involved in the story.

I. BEFORE YOU READ

Take a moment to create your own first impression of "Super-duper-cold Saturdays."

1. With a partner, talk about what the words in the Story Impression mean.
2. Then talk about what the story might be about. Write sentences using each word on the left.
3. After you've read "Super-duper-cold Saturdays," look again at this Story Impression. Think about how accurate your guess about the story was.

Story Impression

MY GUESS ABOUT THE STORY

EXAMPLE

frozen Everything outside was completely frozen

stupid

zillion

thermostat

Jack Frost

couch

Momma

juvenile delinquent

cool

choice

II. READ

Now read "Super-duper-cold Saturdays."

1. As you read, try to **visualize** the scene being described.
2. Make sketches of the scene that you "see."

Response Notes

"Super-duper-cold Saturdays" from *The Watsons Go to Birmingham—1963* by Christopher Paul Curtis

It was one of those super-duper-cold Saturdays. One of those days that when you breathed out, your breath kind of hung frozen in the air like a hunk of smoke and you could walk along and look exactly like a train blowing out big, fat, white puffs of smoke.

EXAMPLE:

It was so cold that if you were stupid enough to go outside, your eyes would automatically blink a thousand times all by themselves, probably so the juice inside of them wouldn't freeze up. It was so cold that if you spit, the slob would be an ice cube before it hit the ground. It was about a zillion degrees below zero.

It was even cold inside our house. We put sweaters and hats and scarves and three pairs of socks on and still were cold. The thermostat was turned all the way up and the furnace was banging and sounding like it was about to blow up, but it still felt like Jack Frost had moved in with us.

All of my family sat real close together on the couch under a blanket. Dad said this would

VOCABULARY

automatically—not consciously or with one's own free will.
thermostat—device in a heating system that responds to temperature changes.

generate a little heat but he didn't have to tell us this, it seemed like the cold automatically made us want to get together and huddle up. My little sister, Joetta, sat in the middle and all you could see were her eyes because she had a scarf wrapped around her head. I was next to her, and on the outside was my mother.

Double-entry Journal

Write how the following quote makes you feel.

Quote	My thoughts
". . .it still felt like Jack Frost had moved in with us."	

Momma was the only one who wasn't born in Flint, so the cold was coldest to her. All you could see were her eyes too, and they were shooting bad looks at Dad. She always blamed him for bringing her all the way from Alabama to Michigan, a state she called a giant icebox. Dad was bundled up on the other side of Joey, trying to look at anything but Momma. Next to Dad, sitting with a little space between them, was my older brother, Byron.

Byron had just turned thirteen, so he was officially a teenage juvenile delinquent and didn't think it was "cool" to touch anybody or let anyone touch him, even if it meant he froze to death. Byron had tucked the blanket

VOCABULARY

generate—create.
Flint—a city in Michigan.
juvenile delinquent—young person guilty of criminal behavior.

"Super-duper-cold Saturdays" continued

Response Notes

between him and Dad down into the cushion of the couch to make sure he couldn't be touched.

Double-entry Journal

Copy a quote from the story that you think is interesting. Write your thoughts about it.

Quote	My thoughts

Dad turned on the TV to try to make us forget how cold we were but all that did was get him in trouble. There was a special news report on Channel 12 telling about how bad the weather was and Dad groaned when the guy said, "If you think it's cold now, wait until tonight, the temperature is expected to drop into record-low territory, possibly reaching the negative twenties! In fact, we won't be seeing anything above zero for the next four to five days!" He was smiling when he said this, but none of the Watson family thought it was funny. We all looked over at Dad. He just shook his head and pulled the blanket over his eyes.

Then the guy on TV said, "Here's a little something we can use to brighten our spirits and give us some hope for the future: The

VOCABULARY

cushion—soft pillow.

temperature in Atlanta, Georgia, is forecast to reach . . ."

Dad coughed real loud and jumped off the couch to turn the TV off but we all heard the weatherman say, ". . . the mid-seventies!" The guy might as well have tied Dad to a tree and said, "Ready, aim, fire!"

"Atlanta!" Momma said. "That's a hundred and fifty miles from home!"

"Wilona . . ." Dad said.

"I knew it," Momma said. "I knew I should have listened to Moses Henderson!"

"Who?" I asked.

Dad said, "Oh Lord, not that sorry story. You've got to let me tell about what happened with him."

Momma said, "There's not a whole lot to tell, just a story about a young girl who made a bad choice. But if you do tell it, make sure you get all the facts right."

We all huddled as close as we could get because we knew Dad was going to try to make us forget about being cold by cutting up. Me and Joey started smiling right away, and Byron tried to look cool and bored.

Double-entry Journal

Find and copy a quote that you think is interesting. Then explain your thoughts about it.

Quote	My thoughts

"Super-duper-cold Saturdays" continued

Response Notes

"Kids," Dad said, "I almost wasn't your father. You guys came real close to having a clown for a daddy named Hambone Henderson . . . ."

"Daniel Watson, you stop right there. You're the one who started that 'Hambone' nonsense. Before you started that, everyone called him his Christian name, Moses. And he was a respectable boy too, he wasn't a clown at all."

"But the name stuck, didn't it? Hambone Henderson. Me and your granddaddy called him that because the boy had a head shaped just like a hambone, had more knots and bumps on his head than a dinosaur. So as you guys sit here giving me these dirty looks because it's a little chilly outside, ask yourselves if you'd rather be a little cool or go through life being known as the Hambonettes."

VOCABULARY

respectable—good; well behaved.
hambone—bone of a ham.

journal entry

What impression do you have of this family?

III. GATHER YOUR THOUGHTS

A. DESCRIBE A SETTING Writers create a setting by using descriptive words and phrases. Skim through the selection again and pay attention to the descriptive words Curtis uses.

1. Find at least 2 words or phrases from the story to write in each box.
2. Then add 1 or 2 other words or phrases of your own.

B. CREATE A SETTING Brainstorm a list of possible settings for a story you will start later.

1. Write about 3 possible places, times, and moods.
2. Circle the one that appeals to you most. Write at least 1 word to describe it in each of the 5 boxes.

Setting 1

time

place

mood

Setting 2

time

place

mood

Setting 3

time

place

mood

Descriptive Words and Phrases

SOUND	SIGHT	FEELING	TASTE	TOUCH

IV. WRITE

Now write a **descriptive paragraph** of the setting of a story you will begin in the next lesson.

1. Use descriptive language in your paragraph to help your readers "see" the time and place.
2. Try to create a mood with your setting.
3. Use the Writers' Checklist to help you revise.

WRITERS' CHECKLIST

CONFUSING WORDS

- ❑ **Did you use *affect* and *effect* correctly? Use *affect* to mean "to influence" and *effect* to mean "the result."**
  EXAMPLES: *Joetta's giggle affected the whole family. Her laughter had a calming effect.*
- ❑ **Did you use *accept* and *except* correctly? *Accept* means "to receive or believe," and *except* means "other than."**
  EXAMPLES: *His mother accepted his apology, but she wondered why no one except him had been naughty.*

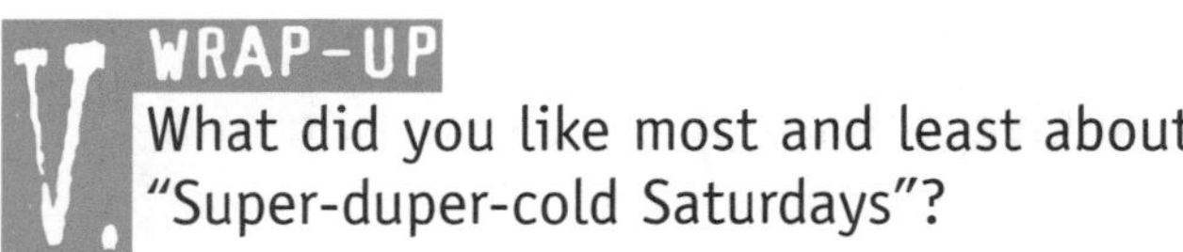

V. WRAP-UP

What did you like most and least about "Super-duper-cold Saturdays"?

READERS' CHECKLIST

ENJOYMENT

- ❑ Did you like the reading?
- ❑ Was the reading experience pleasurable?
- ❑ Would you want to reread the piece or recommend it to someone?

24: New Kids

How difficult is it to be the new kid? When you read stories, do you ever ask yourself, "How would I feel if this were me?" Asking questions as you read can help you develop a strong connection with the reading.

I. BEFORE YOU READ

To begin thinking about "New Kids," read a few sentences from the selection.

1. With a partner, decide which sentence comes first, which comes next, and so on. Number them.
2. Then make some predictions about the story.

Think-pair-share

____ "I knew that God had finally gotten sick of me being teased and picked on all the time."

____ "I got on the bus and took the seat right behind the driver."

____ "The worst part about being teased was riding the school bus on those mornings when Byron and Buphead decided they were going to skip school."

____ "Whenever someone new started coming to Clark, most of the kids took some time to see what he was like."

____ "The bus was real quiet. We'd never seen the driver get this mad before."

I predict this story will be about:

My partner predicts:

II. READ

Now read "New Kids" carefully.

1. Pay special attention to how the author describes a problem and then resolves it.
2. As you read, use the Response Notes to **predict** what will happen next.

Response Notes

EXAMPLE:
Those boys will do something mean.

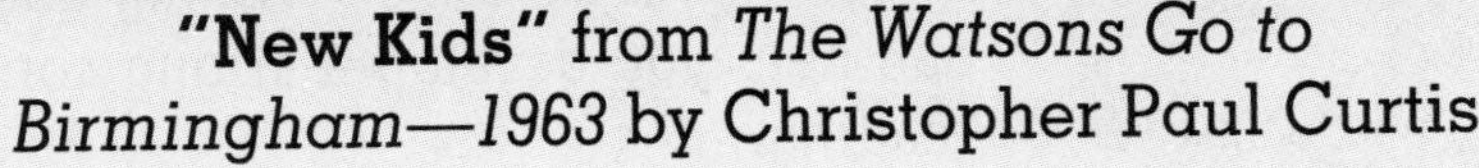

"New Kids" from *The Watsons Go to Birmingham—1963* by Christopher Paul Curtis

The worst part about being teased was riding the school bus on those mornings when Byron and Buphead decided they were going to skip school.

We'd be standing on the corner waiting for the bus, Byron, Buphead and all the other old thugs in one bunch, Larry Dunn, Banky and all the other young thugs in another bunch, the regular kids like Joetta in a third bunch and me off to the side by myself. When we saw the bus about three blocks away, we all got in a line—old thugs, young thugs, regular kids, then me. It wasn't until the bus stopped and the door opened that I knew whether By and Buphead were going. I hated it when By walked past and said, "Give my regards to Clark, Poindexter." Some of the time those words were like a signal for the other kids to jump on me.

But the day I stopped hating the bus so much began with those same words. We were all lined up. "Give my regards to Clark, Poindexter," By said, and disappeared around the bus's back. I got on the bus and took the seat right behind the driver. The days By rode, I

VOCABULARY

thugs—rough people; bullies.

"New Kids" continued

Response Notes

would sit a few rows from him in the back, on other days the driver was the most protection.

stop+clarify

Why does Poindexter, the narrator, hate riding the bus?

stop+clarify

The bus drove down into public housing, and after everyone was picked up we headed toward Clark. But today the bus driver did something he'd never done before. He noticed two kids running up late . . . and he stopped to let them get on. Every other time someone was late, he'd just laugh at them and tell the rest of us, "This is the only way you little punks is gonna learn to be punctual. I hope that fool has a pleasant walk to school." Then no matter how hard the late kid banged on the side of the bus, the driver would just take off, laughing out of the window.

That was part one of my miracle, that let me know something special was going to happen. As soon as the doors for the bus swung open and two strange new boys got on, part two of my miracle happened.

stop+predict

What do you think the second part of the miracle will be?

stop+predict

VOCABULARY

punctual—on time.

Every once in a while, Momma would make me go to Sunday school with Joey. Even though it was just a bunch of singing and coloring in coloring books and listening to Mrs. Davidson, I had learned one thing. I learned about getting saved. I learned how someone could come to you when you were feeling real, real bad and could take all of your problems away and make you feel better. I learned that the person who saved you, your personal saver, was sent by God to protect you and to help you out.

When the bigger one of the two boys who got on the bus late said to the driver in a real down-South accent, "Thank you for stopping, sir," I knew right away. I knew that God had finally gotten sick of me being teased and picked on all the time.

As I looked at this new boy with the great big smile and the jacket with holes in the sleeves and the raggedy tennis shoes and the tore-up blue jeans, I knew who he was. Maybe he didn't live a million years ago and maybe he didn't have a beard and long hair and maybe he wasn't born under a star but I knew anyway, I knew God had finally sent me some help, I knew God had finally sent me my personal saver!

stop+question

In what way is this new boy Poindexter's "personal saver"?

Response Notes

As soon as the boy thanked the driver in that real polite, real country way, I jerked around in my seat to see what the other kids were going to do to him. Whenever someone new started coming to Clark, most of the kids took some time to see what he was like. The boys would see if he was tough or weak, if he was cool or a square, and the girls would look to see if he was cute or ugly. Then they decided how to treat him.

I knew they weren't going to waste any time with this new guy, it was going to be real easy and real quick with him. He was like nobody we'd seen before. He was raggedy, he was country, he was skinny, and he was smiling at everybody a mile a minute. The boy with him had to be his little brother; he looked like a shrunk-up version of the big one.

Everyone had stopped what they were doing and were real quiet. Some were standing up to get a better look. The older one got an even bigger smile on his face and waved real hard at everybody, the little shrunk-up version of him smiled and did the same thing. Then they said, "Hiya, y'all!" and I knew that here was someone who was going to be easier for the kids to make fun of than me!

Most of the kids were just staring. Then Larry Dunn said, "Lord today, look at the nappy-headed, downhome, country corn flake the cat done drugged up from Mississippi, y'all!" About a million fingers pointed at the

new kids and a million laughs almost knocked them over.

Larry Dunn threw an apple core from the back of the bus and the new kid got his hand up just in time to block it from hitting him in the face. Little bits of apple exploded all over the kid, his brother and me. The other kids went wild laughing and saying to each other, "Hiya, y'all!"

The bus driver jumped out of his seat and stood between the new kid and Larry Dunn.

"You see? You see how you kids is? This boy shows some manners and some respect and y'all want to attack him, that's why not one of y'all's ever gonna be nothin'!" The bus driver was really mad. "Larry Dunn, you better sit . . . down and cut this mess out. I know you don't want to start panning on folks, do you? Not with what I know 'bout your momma."

stop+summarize

What causes the bus driver to fly into such a rage?

stop+summarize

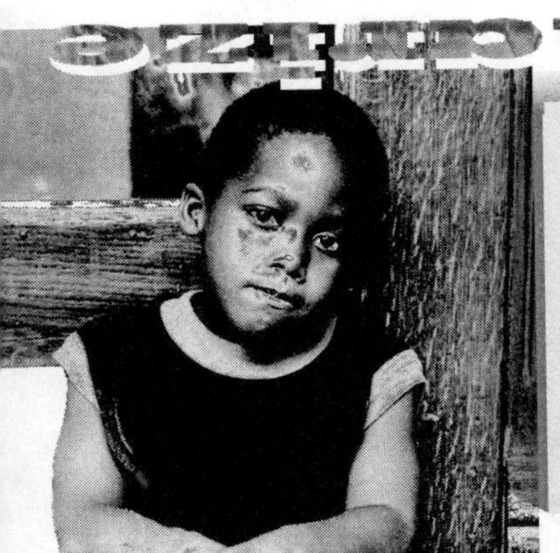

Someone said, "Ooh!" and Larry sat down. The bus was real quiet. We'd never seen the driver get this mad before. He pushed the two new kids into the same seat as me and told

VOCABULARY
panning—criticizing.

"New Kids" continued

Response Notes

them, "Don't you pay no mind to them little fools, they ain't happy lest they draggin' someone down." Then he had to add, "Y'all just sit next to Poindexter, he don't bother no one."

I sat there and looked at them sideways. I didn't say anything to them and they didn't say anything to me. But I was kind of surprised that God would send a saver to me in such raggedy clothes.

With a reading partner, fill in this organizer to show what happens in "New Kids." Give as much detail as you can.

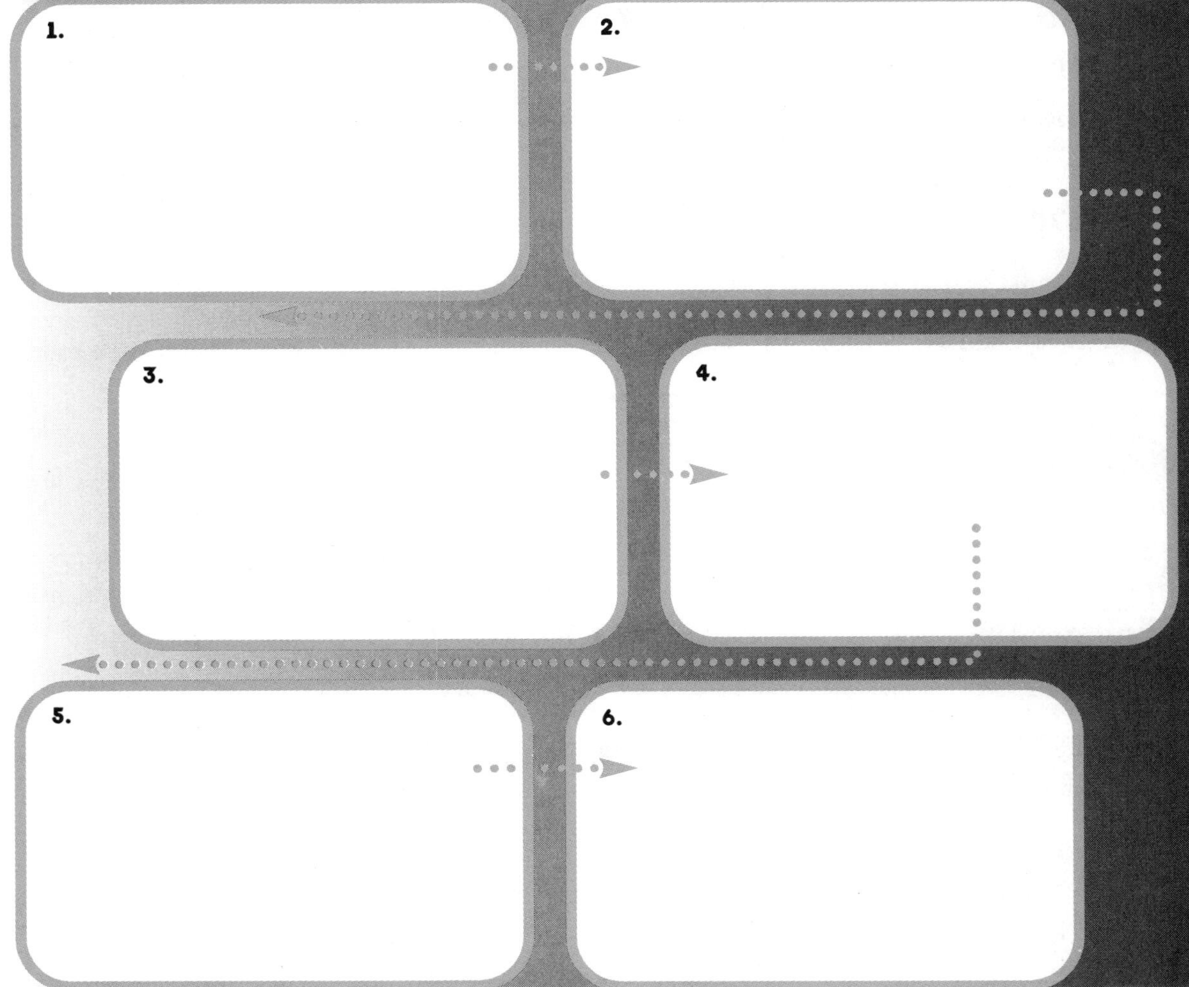

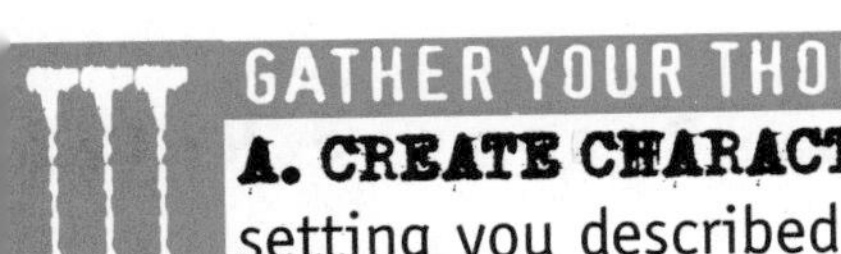

III. GATHER YOUR THOUGHTS

A. CREATE CHARACTERS Now look back at the setting you described on pages 226-227.

1. Think about using that setting in the beginning of a story.
2. On the lines below, make a list of the characters you want to include in your story. Next to each character's name, write a brief description.

character name:	description:
1. character name:	description:
2. character name:	description:
3. character name:	description:

B. PLAN Use this Story Map to plan your story.

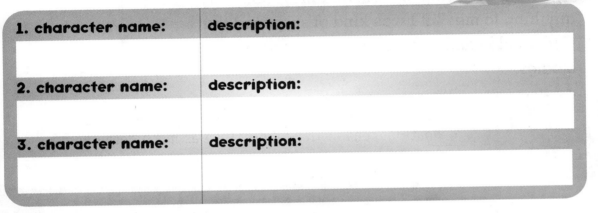

Story Map

1. THE SITUATION

2. A PROBLEM DEVELOPS.

3. THINGS GET WORSE.

4. A POSSIBLE ANSWER APPEARS.

5. THE PROBLEM IS SOLVED.

6. THE END.

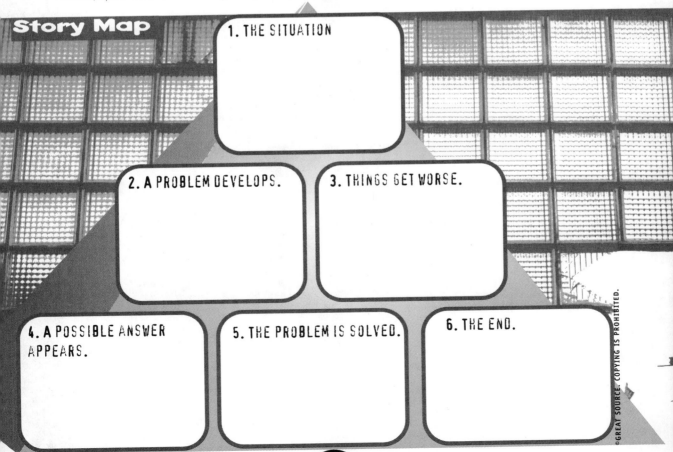

IV. WRITE

Now write a **story beginning** that goes with the setting you described on page 226.

1. Use your notes to help you get started.
2. Draft the first part of your story here. (Rewrite a second draft of your story after your revise it.)
3. Look at the Writers' Checklist to help you revise.

WRITERS' CHECKLIST

EASILY CONFUSED WORDS

- ❑ **Did you correctly use the words *to, too,* and *two*?**
  EXAMPLES: *Jennifer was too tired to go. Robert worked with two friends.*
- ❑ **Did you correctly use the words *than* and *then*?**
  EXAMPLES: *He's a better tennis player than I am. First, the conductor bowed, and then the musicians stood up.*

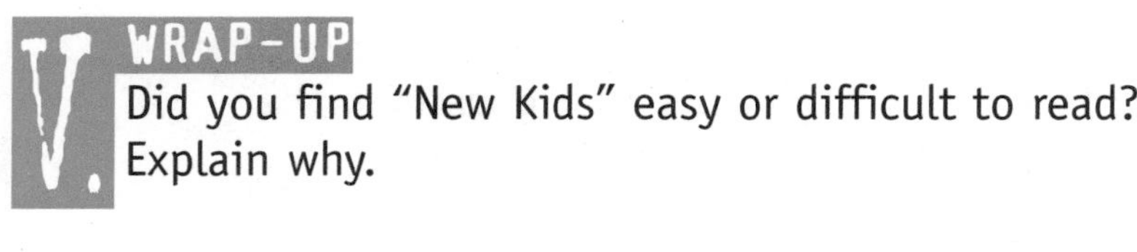

V. WRAP-UP

Did you find "New Kids" easy or difficult to read? Explain why.

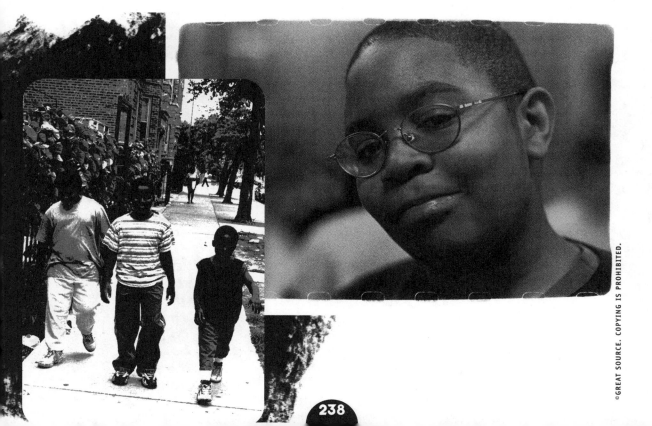

READERS' CHECKLIST

EASE

- ❑ Was the passage easy to read?
- ❑ Were you able to read it smoothly and without difficulty?

Acknowledgments

8 "I'm Nobody," by Emily Dickinson. Reprinted by permission of the publishers and the trustees of Amherst College from THE POEMS OF EMILY DICKINSON, Thomas H. Johnson, ed., Cambridge, MA: The Belknap Press of Harvard University Press, copyright © 1951, 1955, 1983 by the President and Fellows of Harvard College.
10 "My Hard Repair Job," from WHEN I DANCE by James Berry. Copyright © 1991 James Berry.
13 "The Turtle," from JIM BISHOP: REPORTER by Jim Bishop. Copyright © 1965 by Jim Bishop. Reprinted by permission of Random House, Inc.
22 "Thank You Ma'am," from SHORT STORIES by Langston Hughes. Copyright 1996 by Ramona Bass and Arnold Rampersad. Reprinted by permission of Hill and Wang, a division of Farrar, Straus and Giroux, LLC.
35 "Caring for the Wounded," by Clara Barton.
44 "The President's Been Shot," from THE DAY LINCOLN WAS SHOT by Richard Bak. © 1998 by Richard Bak.
53, 55 "Toby Boyce" and "Gideon Adams," from BULL RUN by Paul Fleischman. Copyright © 1993 by Paul Fleischman.
62, 64 "Shem Suggs" and "Judah Jenkins," from BULL RUN by Paul Fleischman. Copyright © 1993 by Paul Fleischman.
71 "A Moment in the Sun Field," by William Brohaugh.
77 "The One Sitting There," by Joanna H. Woś. "The One Sitting There" originally appeared in THE MALAHAT REVIEW #86 © 1989 by Joanna H. Woś. Reprinted by permission of Joanna H. Woś.
84 "Pandora," by Bernard Evslin, from THE GREEK GODS by Bernard Evslin et al. Copyright © 1966 by Scholastic Inc.; copyright renewed 1994. Reprinted by permission.
95 "Hera," by Ingri and Edgar Parin d'Aulaire, from D'AULAIRE'S BOOK OF GREEK MYTHS by Ingri & Edgar Parin d'Aulaire. Copyright © 1962 by Ingri and Edgar Parin d'Aulaire. Used by permission of Random House Children's Books, a division of Random House, Inc.
105, 119 "Arrival," by John Christopher, from WHEN THE TRIPODS CAME by John Christopher. © 1988 by John Christopher. Used by permission of Dutton Children's Books, a division of Penguin Putnam, Inc.
132 "Life Doesn't Frighten Me," by Maya Angelou, from AND STILL I RISE by Maya Angelou. Copyright © 1978 by Maya Angelou. Reprinted by permission of Random House, Inc.
138 "Stanley Yelnats," by Louis Sachar, from Chapters 1-3 from HOLES by Louis Sachar. Copyright © 1998 by Louis Sachar. Reprinted by permission of Farrar, Straus and Giroux, LLC.
147 "The Revolt of Denmark Vesey," from IT HAPPENED IN AMERICA by Lila Perl, © 1992 by Lila Perl. Reprinted by permission of Henry Holt and Company, LLC.
156 "Born Into Slavery," by Frederick Douglass.
165 "Nardo," by Victor Martinez, from PARROT IN THE OVEN by Victor Martinez. TEXT COPYRIGHT 1996 BY VICTOR MARTINEZ. Used by permission of HarperCollins Publishers.
174 "Picking," by Victor Martinez, from PARROT IN THE OVEN by Victor Martinez TEXT COPYRIGHT 1996 BY VICTOR MARTINEZ. Used by permission of HarperCollins Publishers.
185 "The Story of My Body," by Judith Ortiz Cofer.
197 "Child of the Americas" by Aurora Levins Morales, from GETTING HOME ALIVE by Aurora Levins Morales and Rosario Morales. Published by Firebrand Books, Ithaca, NY. © 1986 by Aurora Levins Morales and Rosario Morales.
203 "The War Arrives," from THE UPSTAIRS ROOM by Johanna Reiss. Copyright © 1972 by Johanna Reiss.
212 "Disaster at Sea," from JOHN F. KENNEDY AND THE PT-109, by Richard Tregaskis. Copyright © 1962 by Richard Tregaskis. Copyright renewed 1990 by Moanna Tregaskis. Reprinted by permission of Random House Children's Books, a division of Random House, Inc.
221 "Super-duper-cold Saturdays," by Christopher Paul Curtis, from THE WATSONS GO TO BIRMINGHAM—1963 by Christopher Paul Curtis. Copyright © 1995 by Christopher Paul Curtis. Used by permission of Delacorte Press, a division of Random House, Inc.
230 "New Kids" by Christopher Paul Curtis, from THE WATSONS GO TO BIRMINGHAM—1963 by Christopher Paul Curtis. Copyright © 1995 by Christopher Paul Curtis. Used by permission of Delacorte Press, a division of Random House, Inc.

Photography:

COVER: All photos © Eileen Ryan.

TABLE OF CONTENTS and INTRODUCTION: All photos © Eileen Ryan except where noted. Page 3:center—courtesy Library of Congress. Page 5: left—courtesy Library of Congress. Page 10: center—courtesy Library of Congress.

CHAPTER 1: All photos ©Eileen Ryan except where noted. Page 11: top—courtesy Library of Congress. Page 12: top—courtesy Library of Congress. Pages 15, 21–22, 25, 27–32: courtesy Library of Congress.

CHAPTER 2: All photos courtesy Library of Congress.

CHAPTER 3: All photos courtesy Library of Congress except where noted. Page 65: lower right—© Eileen Ryan. Page 66: upper right—© Eileen Ryan.

CHAPTER 4: All photos © Eileen Ryan except where noted. Pages 77, 80: Photodisc.

CHAPTER 5: All photos © Eileen Ryan except where noted. Page 83: upper right—courtesy Library of Congress. Page 83: upper left and Page 84: inset—© North Wind Picture Archives. Page 89: Photodisc. Page 99: inset—courtesy Library of Congress. Page 101: center—courtesy Library of Congress.

CHAPTER 6: All photos © Eileen Ryan except where noted. Page 104: upper right—courtesy NASA. Page 105: courtesy Library of Congress. Page 107: courtesy NASA. Pages 118–119, 122: courtesy Library of Congress. Page 123: background—courtesy NASA. Page 127: inset—courtesy NASA. Pages 128–129: courtesy NASA.

CHAPTER 7: All photos courtesy Library of Congress except where noted. Page 131: top—Photodisc.

Acknowledgments continued

Page 132: upper right—© Eileen Ryan. 133–135: background—© Eileen Ryan.

CHAPTER 8: All photos courtesy Library of Congress except where noted. Pages 146, 148–151, 154, 158, 162: backgrounds—© Eileen Ryan.

CHAPTER 9: All photos courtesy Library of Congress except where noted. Pages 164-166, 169, 171: © Eileen Ryan.

CHAPTER 10: All photos © Eileen Ryan except where noted. Page 183: bottom—courtesy Library of Congress. Page 188: bottom—courtesy Library of Congress. Pahe 198: courtesy Library of Congress.

CHAPTER 11: All photos courtesy Library of Congress except where noted. Page 201: center—courtesy National Archive. Page 209: © Eileen Ryan. Pages 212–213, 217: courtesy National Archive.

CHAPTER 12: All photos © Eileen Ryan except where noted. Page 219: bottom—courtesy Library of Congress. Page 228: insets—courtesy Library of Congress. Page 233: courtesy Library of Congress. Page 237: top—courtesy Library of Congress.

Cover and Book Design: Christine Ronan and Sean O'Neill, Ronan Design

Permissions:
Feldman and Associates

Developed by Nieman Inc.

The editors have made every effort to trace the ownership of all copyrighted selections found in this book and to make full acknowledgment for their use. Omissions brought to our attention will be corrected in a subsequent edition.

Author/Title **Index**